The British
Art Show⁴

Manchester

12 November 1995 – 4 February 1996

Upper Campfield Market, Castlefield
Castlefield Gallery
Chinese Arts Centre
City Art Galleries
Cornerhouse
Metropolitan Galleries
Whitworth Art Gallery

Edinburgh

24 February – 28 April 1996

City Art Centre
Collective Gallery
Fruitmarket Gallery
Royal Botanic Garden
Scottish National Gallery of Modern Art
Stills Gallery
Talbot Rice Gallery

Cardiff

18 May – 21 July 1996

Chapter Arts Centre
Ffotogallery
National Museum of Wales
Oriel Gallery
(in collaboration with St David's Hall and Cardiff Bay Art Trust)

The British
Art Show[4]

National Touring Exhibitions

H. L.

A National Touring Exhibition organised by the Hayward Gallery, London

Presented in association with participating venues in the cities of Manchester, Edinburgh and Cardiff

Manchester showing: **SIEMENS**
Sponsored by Siemens plc

Edinburgh showing: FAULDS · THE SCOTTISH ARTS COUNCIL · Lothian and Edinburgh Enterprise Limited

With additional assistance from Edinburgh District Council, Lothian Regional Council, Esmée Fairbairn Charitable Trust, The Hope Scott Trust and MOMART

Exhibition Organiser: Vicky Lewis, with Katrina Crookall and Andrew Patrizio

Education Co-ordinator: Helen Luckett

Photographs: Hugh Glendinning (pp. 74, 75), Andrew Holligan (pp. 46, 47), Per Hüttner (p. 19), John Riddy (p. 37), Stephen White (cover and pp. 14, 52, 54), Jonty Wilde (p. 71), Gareth Winters (p. 76), Edward Woodman (pp. 47, 51, 28, 36, 60, 61, 62)

Publication designed by Martin Farran-Lee

Printed by White Dove Press

Cover: Damien Hirst **I Love, Love** 1994/95 (detail) (cat. 23)

ISBN 1 85332 145 1

National Touring Exhibitions, Arts Council Collection and Hayward Gallery publications are distributed by Cornerhouse Publications, 70 Oxford Street, Manchester M1 5NH (tel. 0161 237 9662; fax. 0161 237 9664)

Contents

Jordan Baseman

Christine Borland

Mat Collishaw

Tacita Dean

Ceal Floyer

John Frankland

Anya Gallaccio

Douglas Gordon

Damien Hirst

Gary Hume

Permindar Kaur

Steve McQueen

Lucia Nogueira

Chris Ofili

Julie Roberts

Bridget Smith

Georgina Starr

Kerry Stewart

Marcus Taylor

Sam Taylor-Wood

Mark Wallinger

Gillian Wearing

Hermione Wiltshire

Jane and Louise Wilson

Catherine Yass

Foreword

Young British artists are attracting an almost unprecedented level of attention. **The British Art Show 4** arrives, therefore, at a timely moment. The exhibition is the fourth in National Touring Exhibitions' series of shows, which have been held at approximately five-yearly intervals and which have looked at recent British art. Since the first exhibition in 1979, The British Art Show has changed in character, in response to new developments in art and rising public expectations. The show is not, and could never hope to be, a representative survey of contemporary British art – the work of artists in this country embodies too complex a blend of influences, cultures and beliefs for that. It has moved by degrees away from a catholic spread across generations and styles to the presentation of increasingly challenging and innovative work.

The British Art Show 4 is particularly adventurous and was planned from the outset as an exhibition extending across a number of galleries and museums in each of the three cities with which we have formed a partnership. Through the exhibition itself, and through the extensive education programmes in each city, we hope that a wide public will be stimulated and encouraged to look at contemporary art in a new way, and we are especially pleased that the exhibition is the first British Art Show to be shown in England, Scotland and Wales, allowing for new nationwide collaborations between all the participating galleries involved.

The nature of the exhibition has been determined by its selectors, Richard Cork, Rose Finn-Kelcey and Thomas Lawson, and we are extremely grateful to them for the committed and thoughtful way in which they have made their selection. The choice of artists is witness to the strength of their belief that remarkably resonant and exciting work is being done in the UK by a fresh generation of artists, many of them still in their twenties and thirties. Two of the three selectors, Rose Finn-Kelcey and Thomas Lawson, are themselves artists, though that very fact can make the evaluation of fellow artists more exacting than usual.

The idea of spreading **The British Art Show 4** around each city originated in response to the increasing resourcefulness and imagination displayed by artists who have themselves sought new strategies for getting their work out and seen in public. The exhibition has therefore turned into a series of different displays with sharply distinctive characters between which the visitor is invited to travel. We are delighted that in Manchester the exhibition has been a catalyst for Upper Campfield Market, Castlefield, becoming a new and impressive venue for contemporary art, thanks mainly to generous support from Manchester City Art Galleries and Manchester City Council.

The enthusiasm, support and expertise of gallery staff in Manchester, Edinburgh and

Cardiff have made an inevitably complicated and at times hectic gestation period extremely stimulating, and we remain indebted to the collaborative efforts of our colleagues in the host cities, in particular, our three city co-ordinators, Stephen Snoddy, Paul Nesbitt and Christopher Coppock. In the three individual cities we should also like to thank the following: in Manchester – Paul Bayley, Catharine Braithwaite, Lindsay Brooks and Arts About Manchester, Vicky Charnock, Alison Edbury, Richard Gray, Mary Griffiths, Penny Hamilton, Stephen Hodder, Sara Holdsworth, Kate Jesson, Kwong Lee, Aileen McEvoy and North West Arts Board, Mark Purcell, Alison Radovanović, Rud Sawers, Kate Seeckts, Michael Simpson, Alistair Smith, Howard Smith, Jude Sykes, Virginia Tandy, Belinda Tilley, Siobhán Ward and Tim Wilcox; in Edinburgh – Michael Cassin, Richard Calvocoressi, Herbert Coutts, Trevor Cromie, Siobhán Dougherty, Edinburgh District Council, Pat Fisher, Keith Hartley, Bill Hare, Sarah Knox, Lothian Regional Council, Mhairi McKenzie Robinson, Sandra Marwick, Sarah Munro, Graeme Murray, Andrew Nairne and the Scottish Arts Council, Caroline Neil, Dianne Stein, Kate Tregaskis, Jane Warrilow, Angela Wrapson, and Ann-Marie Wagener; in Cardiff – David Alston, Stuart Cameron, Sue Cunningham, Colin Ford, Isabel Hitchman and the Welsh Arts Council, Nigel Meager, Sally Medlyn and Cardiff Bay Arts Trust, Sally Moss, Jenni Spencer-Davies, Michael Tearle, Charles Wilde and Cardiff Arts Marketing. We would also like to acknowledge the encouragement and support of the Arts Council of England, in particular Marjorie Allthorpe-Guyton, Director of Visual Arts, and herself one of The British Art Show selectors in 1984.

Many other individuals have advised and assisted us throughout the development of the project, and we would like to thank the following in particular: Hugh Adams, Emily Ash, Barry Barker, Jon Bewley, Brian Biggs, Lewis Biggs, James Birrell, Martin Boyce, Katrina Brown, Pavel Büchler, James Bustard, Caroline Collier, Andrée Cooke, Janet Currie, David Curtis, Penelope Curtis, Susan Daniel, Yvonne Dean, Jacqueline Donachie, Charles Esche, Alex Farquharson, Stephen Foster, Margot Heller, Stephen Hobson, Robert Hopper, Jay Jopling, Reuben Kench, John Kennedy, Angela Kingston, Alison Lloyd, Elizabeth MacGregor, John Millard, Sandy Moffat, Susan Morgan, Joanne Morehead, Lynda Morris, Richard Salmon, Kim Sweet, Gilane Tawadros, Caroline Taylor, Gary Thomas, Catherine Ugwe, H. Walton, David Ward, Nicolas Ward-Jackson, Jonathan Watkins, and Nicola White.

We would like to thank John Wyver and Illuminations Television for their generous support in creating the innovative multi-media programme which accompanies the exhibition tour and, in general, for their work in extending the boundaries of the exhibition beyond its traditional limits. We are also grateful to Marcelo Spinelli, Mary Alice Stack and Hannah Redler, for their work in preparing education materials.

Much of the new art seen here lies outside the traditional media of painting and sculpture and, as such, has required meticulous planning, installation and maintenance. We are most grateful to the many technicians, art handlers and advisors who have assisted us at every stage, and in particular Jem Legh, Clive Gilman, Eddie Berg and Simon Bradshaw from MITES and Moviola.

We greatly appreciate the support given by Siemens plc, who have sponsored the Manchester showing, and the educational programme in particular. Their commitment to some of the most innovative work being done by young artists will, we are sure, do much to open up the exhibition to a wide public. We should like to thank Alan Wood and Richard Caithness of Siemens for their personal interest in the exhibition.

Numerous colleagues throughout the Hayward Gallery and Royal Festival Hall have assisted in various ways. Susan Ferleger Brades, Deputy Director of Exhibitions, played an invaluable role in guiding our collective efforts. The exhibition would not have been possible without assistance from staff in Exhibitions, Marketing, Development, Design and Finance Departments. We wish particularly to thank our former colleague Alexandra Noble for her contribution at the initial stages of the project; Andrew Patrizio for co-ordinating marketing and contractual arrangements; Helen Luckett for developing the educational programme; Linda Schofield for co-ordinating the publication; Sam Doyle and Alison Wright for organising the marketing and press campaigns.

Finally, and most importantly, we would like to join the selectors in thanking the artists and the lenders for making this exhibition possible.

HENRY MEYRIC HUGHES
Director of Exhibitions

ROGER MALBERT
Head of National Touring Exhibitions

VICKI LEWIS
Exhibition Organiser

RICHARD CORK

Injury time

As the 1990s lurch towards an ignominious close, more and more young artists are becoming preoccupied with a sense of frustration, confinement and loss. In the work they produce, this gathering disquiet spans a range of diverse and unpredictable forms. But an awareness of injury in all its manifestations – whether mental or physical, individual or social, hidden or exposed, self-inflicted or perpetrated by an aggressor – remains the fundamental obsession.

By a paradox, though, the art itself is far from dejected. Humour, albeit of a sardonic kind, abounds. So does the conviction that, however ailing their recession-battered nation may be, young British artists have rarely been more energetic and resourceful. They seize with relish on an ever-expanding array of media, often moving with supple confidence between painting, sculpture, video, photography, film, words and ready-made objects. The old hierarchical allegiances have been replaced by a readiness to cross over, at will, from one way of working to another. This free-wheeling appetite for hybridity is matched by a willingness to exhibit together. Without subscribing to the ethos of a unified group or movement, they are prepared to organise their own mixed shows and generate a mood of interdependent vitality well-seasoned with resilience.

If the old century has worn itself out, and appears ready to expire before the new millennium arrives, these irrepressible artists show no sign of exhaustion. On the contrary, their stubborn determination engenders an atmosphere hectically akin to injury time in football, when every player tries to raise the level of energy as the end approaches. Powered by that final burst of adrenalin, and not knowing when the last whistle will blow, they realise that anything can happen in the dying moments of the game.

Memento Mori

All the same, the artists in this exhibition are by no means reckless. The prevailing mood is cool, alert and interrogative. Some of the participants pursue their interests with the zeal of a detective and present the outcome of their investigations in a precise, even chilling manner. None more clinically than **Damien Hirst**, who insists on confronting us with the brute fact of mortality at every turn.

In Britain, death is still a taboo word. Most of us have a horror of the grave and we seal ourselves off from all contaminating contact with extinction. Euphemisms like 'the departed' linger, testifying to a belief that anyone who clearly acknowledges human dissolution is guilty of inexcusable gloom. Hirst, however, manages to be frank about death without sliding into morbidity. Going even further than the most uncompromising painter of a *vanitas* still life, he presents the viewer with the incontrovertible reality of extinction.

The butterfly's brief lifespan, from hatching to decay, became the subject of an early exhibition called *In and Out of Love*, 1991. Hirst finds beauty in their ephemeral existence, especially when they end up attached to the surface of a deceptively festive painting. But he can be brutal about obliteration as well. He is capable of incorporating an electric fly-killing device in a sculpture, using the classic minimalist form of an austere, empty box and transforming it into a charnel-house.

Hirst forces us to think queasily about the part we play in the extermination process, as well as our own inability to evade the same fate. Unafraid to contemplate the gruesomeness of putrefaction, he placed a rotting cow's head in one of his works – a *memento mori* which, ironically, provided sustenance for the insects inhabiting the same glass container. He is even more interested in preservation. With the detachment of a Victorian taxidermist, he has mounted fish in tanks brimming with

Damien Hirst
**20 He Tried
to Internalise
Everything**
1992-94

formaldehyde, placed them on shelves and mocked their futility by calling them *Isolated Elements Swimming in the Same Direction for the Purpose of Understanding*, 1991. Hirst's mordant wit is most evident in his elaborate, ingenious titles. But he remains, for all his burgeoning notoriety and instinctive talent for showmanship, utterly serious about the need to acknowledge and somehow come to terms with the unfathomable transience of life.

Hirst's preoccupation with cages is reminiscent of the similar structures enclosing the figures in many of Francis Bacon's paintings. But the human presence is hard to detect in his work, except by implication in a work like *The Acquired Inability to Escape*, 1991 where the glass-walled prison encases a desk, chair and brimming ashtray. Like George Stubbs, another British artist who was prepared to study rotting flesh with equanimity, Hirst would rather use animals than images of people.

In this respect, he differs from **Julie Roberts**, a Glasgow-based painter who meditates on the inescapability of death. She has no desire to avoid the silent occupants of a mortuary. Roberts leads us in there, and installs the shrouded corpse in the very centre of a space otherwise relentlessly bare. There is nothing gratuitous about her concentration on cadavers. They remain wrapped in sheets and thereby reflect Roberts' determination to stop short of shocking the viewer with gruesome anatomical revelations.

The formality of body-display inside the morgue invests these anonymous figures with an enigmatic dignity. There they lie, emanating light and, apparently, purged of the wounds or disease that caused them to die. Roberts' paintings are like secular altarpieces. Their devotional aura might suggest an urge on the artist's part to redeem her frozen subjects. However, this supposition sits uneasily with her matter-of-fact handling of pigment, and with the expanse of emptiness encircling each body. The figures are marooned within a void. They float like the animals suspended in Hirst's formaldehyde tanks. The possibility that they might be awaiting a post-mortem reinforces the air of suspense.

Sometimes Roberts adds to our disquiet by pointing out, in a concise subtitle, that the body belongs to a child. She also emphasizes the coldness of the rooms where the bodies are stored. One figure may be wrapped in a scarlet sheet and surrounded by an ample expanse of flat, maroon pigment, but the overall impact is oddly glacial. Other paintings focus on the chilling equipment to be found in similar institutions. The male and female restraining jackets isolated on two canvases are empty, for the moment at least. Their effect on the human body is, however, easy to imagine. An invisible figure seems to haunt the female jacket, while its male counterpart appears to advance with predatory movements towards an unseen patient.

Roberts is also haunted by the oppressive inheritance of the past. Everything that attends us in medical contexts today stems, she implies, from attitudes and prototypes developed through history. Hence her decision to devote one painting to a nineteenth-century dentist's chair, its red plush seating and head-rest doing little to ameliorate the claw-like legs. Preserving such an object in a medical museum might even enhance its sinister aspect, forcing us to appraise it with the detachment Roberts cultivates in all her paintings. Like the surgical equipment ranged on shelves in some of Hirst's work, the apparatus resembles evidence discovered at the scene of crimes centred, for the most part, on people reduced to a state of helplessness by the contraptions enclosing them.

Christine Borland shares this fascination with historical exhibits and uses the conventions of museum display as a means of organising and presenting her work. Compared with Roberts' impeccably crafted paintings, though, Borland's approach is deliberately raw. Police museums are far more likely to fascinate her than their medical equivalents. She savours their quirky, home-made character, their freedom from the rules that govern and often stifle related institutions. In her *Black Museum*, 1994 (cat. 5), she introduces a macabre humour which has parallels with Hirst but plays little part in Roberts' art.

The Portakabin housing this bizarre array of exhibits is, for one thing, risibly at odds with the grandiloquence of official museum architecture. Once inside, visitors find themselves wondering at the apparent randomness, even eccentricity, of the exhibits. The notes supplied by Borland as a guide to the Portakabin's contents are sober and, at times, precisely scientific in their willingness to impart detailed information about the type of weapon employed by the criminal, the velocity of a bullet, or the time taken for the victim's blood cells to sink to the lowest part of the corpse. This factual presentation does not, however, detract from the strangeness and unpredictability of the exhibits. At her most direct, Borland displays the bone of an arm fractured during an instinctive attempt to ward off an attack. The skeletal fragment contrasts oddly with the house plants, testifying to the fact that detectives, alerted by the stink of rotting flesh, once found human remains hidden in three large pot plants. Having decanted the pots' contents on to a plastic dustbin lid, they discovered a complete human spine wrapped around the roots.

Grisliness and surreal absurdity coexist in the *Black Museum*, 1994 to a bewildering extent. Borland must have relished her decision to include papier mâché heads on an upper shelf, where they loll like an executioner's decapitated trophies. Although deriving from the 'self-portrait' heads made as decoys by prisoners during escape-bids, they end up looking forlornly comic. The reverse is true of the photographs showing abandoned melons on a stairwell. At first glance, they look inconsequential, the result of a silly accident. But the more these split and spilled fruits are examined, the more sinister they become. The melons may have been left behind after a savage assault, and Borland's notes underline their role as evidence by explaining how droplets, splashes and stains can help in the reconstruction of a criminal incident.

For all her willingness to be blunt in the presentation of objects, Borland would not want to display the melons themselves and leave them to decay in public. For **Anya Gallaccio**, however, the process of putrefaction is a central element in much

Anya Gallaccio
forest floor 1995
Carpet, larch
and trees
Courtesy of Chiltern
Sculpture Trail

of her work. As if to defy art's immemorial desire for permanence, she is prepared to lay out fruit in an exhibition and let it rot. No English reticence dilutes the brazenness of her approach to the task. She once unloaded a ton of oranges on to a London warehouse floor, and surrounded them on the walls with silkscreen images of the same fruit. Initially, the correspondence between the real fruit and their pictures was complete, presenting the viewer with an overload of information about the appearance, smell and tactile appeal of oranges at their ripest. But as the show proceeded, they started to fester. The disparity between mouldy fruit and gleaming silkscreens became increasingly grotesque. By the end, the oranges had grown almost unrecognisable in their deterioration, and could only be identified with confidence through the images still lustrous on the walls.

In one sense, then, Gallaccio could be described as the most unrelenting artist of her generation, hammering home the ravages inflicted by time with the ruthlessness of a hell-fire preacher. The truth about her attitude, though, is far less melodramatic. While acknowledging the melancholy of decay, she is also captivated by the transformations it engenders. Like the submerged skeleton in Shakespeare's *The Tempest*, which suffers a sea-change 'into something rich and strange', nature's forms undergo in her work a metamorphosis worthy of wonder as well as disgust.

By allowing a compressed host of luminous red gerberas to droop, fade and crinkle in the front window of the Karsten Schubert Gallery, she was not simply delivering a baleful sermon about the withering that awaits us all. Alongside this melancholy demonstration of transience, Gallaccio insisted that putrescence has just as much claim on our attention as health.

Indeed, existing definitions of 'well-being' are called into question by her work. Are we meant to deplore the change undergone by the chocolate in *Stroke*, 1994, an installation which spread the dark brown substance across the gallery walls to a height of about two metres? Or are we invited to accept, even celebrate, the oxidising whiteness which gradually dappled the chocolate's surface? Gallaccio herself leaves the question open. But the real possibility that she may savour the bleaching process lends the work a vital ambiguity, encouraging us to see the inevitability of decomposition in a new and more liberating light.

Uneasy Interiors

Whether real or imagined, rooms inside buildings now provide artists with some of their most disquieting images. In one respect, Gallaccio's *Stroke*, 1994 is dark and enveloping enough to resemble a place of confinement – with more than a suggestion of a prison smeared with a 'dirty protest' by its angry inmates. But **Catherine Yass** has taken the exploration of architectural space much further. Commissioned by the Public Art Development Trust to make a series of images for Springfield Hospital, a rambling psychiatric institution built in the nineteenth century, she intended at first to concentrate on portraits of patients and staff. Yass, however, has never been content to photograph her sitters in isolation. They are always seen in relation to a context which enlarges, and in some cases transforms, their significance. So the hospital backgrounds played a powerful role from the start, and in the end became so engrossing that she produced a sequence of corridors inhabited by no one.

The results, while anchored in Yass's response to specific spaces within Springfield, have a curious universality. Although corridors are associated above all with hospitals, these passages could be found in schools, factories or any of the other large institutional structures erected by the Victorians. Their impact is complex. Sometimes the narrowness is claustrophobic, and the feeling of constriction reinforced by exposed ducts bearing down from the ceiling. Elsewhere, though, oppressiveness gives way to a more hallucinatory alternative. Yass's medium is the light-box and she exploits its peculiar radiance to the hilt. The reflectiveness of the gloss-painted walls takes on a strangely shimmering quality; exposed light bulbs appear to suffuse their surroundings with an orange glow; and distant doors emit a pulsating electric blue.

Catherine Yass
86 From **Corridors**
1995

This, the most ubiquitous of all Yass's heightened, acidic colours, can spread across the floor as well. The blue makes one corridor appear unaccountably flooded, adding to the mood of expectancy. But it can also lead to frustration. For the corridors remain vacant, often terminating in doors that deny us entry to the rooms beyond. Occasionally, the blueness seems to hint at transparency, offering the promise of imminent access. Light presses through from the other side, enlivening the gaps between door and floor with enticing lines of brightness. In the end, however, they tantalise us with their allure. The promised revelation is withheld and we are left contemplating the implacability of labyrinths that terminate, elsewhere, in the cheerless solidity of a bare wall.

If Yass's light-saturated stillness sometimes stirs memories of pellucid skies in radiant quattrocento panels, **Bridget Smith**'s photographs seem even more related to the experience offered by paintings. At art college she worked for a while as a minimalist painter, and the seductiveness of colour at its most sumptuous provides her extended series of cinema images with their initial appeal. They are, on the face of it, far more beguiling than Yass's corridors. Ample enough in size to make us feel we have entered the auditoria, they further imply a vantage cosseted by the comfort of a seat near the front. From here, we are encouraged to gaze leisurely at the sheen and texture of the thickly folded curtains, burnished by lighting intense enough to give their resplendent fabrics the promise of incipient pleasure.

The revelation is never fulfilled. After a while the repetitive emphasis on closed curtains, in photograph after photograph, becomes eerie. So does the absence of an audience. Are we witnessing the moment before a performance, the end, or the final stage in the life of the cinema itself? The potent titles of these images – *Curzon, Odeon, Coronet* and *Empire* – evoke a distant era when a night at the movies was an opulent experience unthreatened by multi-screen uniformity and the rivalrous growth of television. But, by concentrating so steadily on emptiness and inactivity, Smith implies that something has gone wrong.

For all their irresistible panache, these interiors rebuff as much as they seduce. Desire is quickened only to be thwarted. The curtains gradually become more defensive than inviting. Always viewed head-on, from a central position that relates Smith to some contemporary German photographers, they refuse to expose what lies behind. Denial of access is even stronger than in Yass's corridor images. In her other work, Smith explores the curious deadness of an unoccupied television game-show studio, or an equally deserted betting shop where nobody seems to believe in the possibility of a win. The despondency of these images may be hidden by dream-inducing glamour in the cinema series, but her underlying toughness should not be doubted.

Although he constructs real spaces rather than making photographs of unattainable interiors, **John Frankland** shows a similar ability to lead us into a deceptively soothing interior. Visitors to *You Can't Touch This*, 1993, his elaborate installation at the Hales Gallery in Deptford, might have imagined that they had stumbled, by mistake, on the office of a smart advertising agency. The room was transformed into a streamlined foyer. An artificial ceiling, low-slung and studded with circular lights, replaced the normal architecture and, along the entire stretch of the wide left wall, Frankland installed a gleaming golden lift.

It remains a beguiling spectacle. Walking alongside, we find ourselves reflected in its surface. Our blurred forms draw us towards the lift and we move nearer in the hope of sharpening the mirror-image. But Frankland frustrates our desire. Faces stay fuzzy even close-to and the lift doors remain resolutely shut. By robbing the machine of its function, Frankland invites us to look at the whole shining apparatus in a new way. However hard we may press the moulded buttons flanking the doors, they will never open. The gold surfaces take on a mocking character. They hold out the promise of infinite wealth and glamour, only to underline their unavailability.

When Frankland started planning the work in 1992, Britain was mired in recession. So this teasing exhibit, poised between painting, sculpture and architecture, could be seen as a monument to the betrayal of hopes inflated beyond all reason in the previous decade. The meaning is reinforced by the material, too. Peer at the lift, and you will soon discover that its air of luxury is superficial. Frankland has made the work by stretching a skin of metalised polyester across the entire surface. It is even cheaper than the supporting wooden frame, and the occasional tiny crease reveals the skin for what it really is.

The tantalising game continues in *Untitled (Shed)*, 1994 (cat. 15). Here Frankland displays a far shinier structure. As its bracketed name indicates, it resembles an ordinary garden shack. But a tour round the sides discloses that it is no more useful than the lift. For this shed has been sealed tight and its bright polyester coating ensures that walls, door and roof are all invaded by clear reflections of the surroundings. Our own presence is mirrored vividly, making the shed seem even more mysterious and impenetrable. We are left wondering why it is so out-of-bounds. Was toxic waste discovered there, or the victim of a crime? Frankland tempts us to speculate, but provides no answers. All we do know is that the shed remains profoundly unsettling.

This strange sense of unease even permeates the work of **Marcus Taylor**, whose perspex sculptures could hardly be more purged and refined. His starting-points are fridges and freezers, so the overall mood should be reassuringly domestic. The more we gaze at these white presences, though, the less familiar they become. Taylor has sanded all the perspex surfaces, so that they no longer offer clear views into the sculptures. We can see only a series of misty, frozen voids, waiting to be filled.

Like Frankland, Taylor ensures that no doors provide a way into his glacial structures. Although one or two are open at the top, access is difficult. So they simply stand there, asking to be admired for their bleached, contemplative beauty. After a while, serenity is replaced by a more sinister mood. It seems to recall the grim story, recently reported in the press, of a youth found dead in a shop freezer by his appalled employer. No reason was given for the tragedy, but it chimes all too well with the disturbing rise in suicides among young British men. So however calmly Taylor's sculptures evoke a world of eternal preservation, they also bear an unnerving resemblance to chambers of extinction.

If a viewer ever gained access to one of Taylor's larger works, the experience would be still more disconcerting. Along with the claustrophobia inherent in occupying such a limited space, the inability to see the world vaguely glimmering outside their sanded surfaces could quickly lead to intense frustration. But Taylor is a subtle artist and he shows no inclination to let his enigmatic art be dominated by negative emotions. Hence his decision, in an ambitious proposal for an installation visitors can enter, to replace tantalising opacity with an extraordinary alternative.

Like Yass's work at Springfield, his proposal centres on a corridor. But Taylor's would be made of steel and positioned on the third floor of a disused industrial building. Access to the corridor is gained from a steel box rising from floor to ceiling, so darkness prevails at this stage. Daylight is visible at the end of the passage, however. Here the visitor discovers another corridor, this time made entirely of glass. Projecting around three metres from the building, it initiates a change from heaviness and solidity to lightness and transparency. The glass corridor, suspended some twelve metres from the ground, offers multiple views of the city outside. In this respect, the mistiness of Taylor's perspex sculptures has given way to clarity and revelation; but the sensation of standing apparently unsupported in space is also disorientating, and the glass box inevitably promotes an awareness of containment and isolation. Once again, an interior offers the promise of discovery and yet ends up denying its pleasurable fulfilment.

Staying Alive

As for the people who occupy interior spaces, they often appear to endure an enforced state of inactivity. In the aptly named *Killing Time*, 1994 (cat. 66), **Sam Taylor-Wood** presents a video installation stiflingly concerned with four figures occupying nondescript interiors. They are all young and look listless. Each one seems alone, dominating the image projected on to a wall. None appears conscious of the presence, on a neighbouring wall, of another figure. They all lead separate existences, united only by the boredom of a world where nothing ever happens – apart from the sound of an intensely charged opera issuing from powerful speakers.

Taylor-Wood offers no clues as to the cause of their malaise. She leaves us to speculate about unemployment, or the state of a generation unsustained by any overriding faith in the future. So, when each of these figures suddenly begins to lip-synch the singers in the opera, the effect is startling. Judging by the movement of their mouths, they know the libretto well. But that does not lessen the strangeness of the exercise. The disparity between the impassioned voices of the performers, and the mundane blend of tedium and anxiety emitted by the people in the videos, could hardly be more acute. Their precise knowledge of the libretto argues that they feel involved with the opera, awakening their potential for engagement to a greater extent, perhaps, than anything else in their lives. Even so, the gap separating them from the singers' heightened emotions remains unbridgeable. *Killing Time*, 1994 leaves us, finally, with a forlorn sense of yearning, of latent aspirations obliged to remain unrealised.

Sam Taylor-Wood
Still from
67 **Brontosaurus**
1995

Taylor-Wood is fascinated by the challenge of bringing together high and low art in this unlikely way. Opera at its most elevated, luxuriously dependent on a highly-trained army of performers, orchestral musicians and stage staff, is combined here with a documentary medium which is relatively cheap and simple to deploy. Yoking them together could be merely laughable, but the outcome is at once challenging and unsettling. The operatic dimension enlarges our understanding of the dilemma confronting these four people – just as the overlay of Samuel Barber's *Adagio for Strings* in Taylor-Wood's *Brontosaurus*, 1995 (cat. 67) transforms the meaning of a naked man's dance. If we could switch off the orchestral sound, and hear the jungle techno which inspired his movements, he would undoubtedly seem more lighthearted and spontaneous. But the classical backing makes his dance measured, and lends his gestures a sombreness unexpectedly reminiscent of a martyred saint in a Renaissance altarpiece.

On a superficial level, **Jane and Louise Wilson**'s video installation *Hypnotic Suggestion "505"*, 1993 (cat. 78) is akin to *Killing Time*, 1994. Two young women sit in a room, their limp bodies initially suggesting that they have abandoned themselves to torpor. There, however, the resemblance between the works ends. For the figures in Jane and Louise Wilson's video are the artists themselves and their sleepiness has been induced by a professional hypnotist unseen by the camera. Moreover, the notion of lifting minds and bodies into a state of suspension was enhanced, at the original Lisson Gallery showing, by the work's setting. Framed in a doorway supported by a flight of altar-like steps, *Hypnotic Suggestion "505"*, 1993 had a highly theatrical and quasi-religious presence. The work also possesses a built-in ability to mesmerise. Both dressed soberly, against an institutional blue curtain, the artists sink back on black leather chairs. They submit by degrees to the hypnotist's slow, soothing, almost priestly voice. And part of the video's fascination lies in the spectacle of two young women abandoning themselves to a calm yet deeply manipulative male authority.

The main drama, though, centres on the artists' reactions to their god-like instructor. They are twins and, having fallen into a trance with surprising rapidity, they echo each other's movements throughout. One of them is quicker than her sister, especially when commanded to raise her hand to her face; but on the whole a sense of uncanny uniformity prevails. They are turned from individuals into marionettes, silently obeying their master's lulling injunction to feel 'restful, peaceful'.

Ultimately, however, the video leaves us with an enigma. Did the hypnosis impose on the artists a regressive pattern of identical behaviour, or bring out an underlying sameness which they prefer to avoid when awake? The answer is not provided: the faithful recording of the session only deals with the surface of the artists' experiences. We are given no inkling of how their minds behaved during the hypnosis and, at the end, the camera zooms in slowly on the curtain until the entire screen is filled with a mysterious, gently pulsating expanse of blue.

In their photographic work, Jane and Louise Wilson explore more disturbing psychological states. Based for the most part on their flat in King's Cross, the images present rooms within rooms and suggest, through the careful use of unpredictable camera angles, cinematic lighting and above all props, that the threatening incidents have either just occurred or are about to erupt. By refusing to spell out the exact source of the ominous mood, the artists invite us to project our own interpretations on to their *mise-en-scène*. They also clearly relish the breaking-down of boundaries between art and their own lives. We cannot tell how far Jane and Louise Wilson feed off the reality of day-to-day existence, but we can be fairly confident that these interiors offer visceral and often dream-like meditations on domestic confinement in contemporary Britain. As in Hirst's cages, Francis Bacon's cell-like spaces emerge as a native precedent for Jane and Louise Wilson's images of entrapment.

While Jane and Louise Wilson usually provide a detailed construction of a room, implying the departure or arrival of its inhabitants, **Ceal Floyer** closes on a single element and charges it with strangeness. The atmosphere in her work is closer to the ennui of Taylor-Wood's *Killing Time*, 1994 (cat. 66) than the covert violence cultivated so stealthily by Jane and Louise Wilson. But instead of showing large-screen videos of seated figures, Floyer contents herself with a modest projection of thumbs twiddling. In a crowded show where different artists have to compete with one another for attention, her diminutive image might easily be overlooked. Understatement, however, is Floyer's forte. She knows how inappropriate it would be to expand the repetitive thumbs into a grandiose showpiece. The whole point of these eternally restless digits, played on an unending loop, rests in their insignificance. Thumb-twiddling, after all, is a sign of Beckett-like inertia. Bordering on paralysis of the will, it bears directly on the frustration running through the work of so many artists from her generation.

Floyer also shares Samuel Beckett's consciousness of a wryly comic absurdity. Nothing could be more deadpan or banal than our initial glimpse of her *Light Switch*, 1992 (cat. 12), apparently spotlit on a wall. Closer inspection discloses, however, that it is a projected image rather than a solid object. The light-switch has no existence outside the slide lodged so cunningly in Floyer's machine. But somewhere else in the room, a real light-switch must have been turned off in order to give the projected image its own visibility.

Floyer clearly savours the perverse wit involved in setting up such a paradox and, in the tersely-titled *Light*, 1994 (cat. 13), she becomes still more subversive. Only a bright yet solitary light bulb hanging from the ceiling is apparent at first. Other than suggesting a debt to the same appliance dangling in several of Bacon's interiors, it seems utterly mundane. Soon, however, we realise that it has not been switched on. Instead, it is illuminated by four projectors. By training slides of bulb-shaped cut-outs on to its glass surface, they make the real bulb glow with light. Apart from the dry humour involved in devoting so much technological trickery to such a nonsensical end, Floyer shows a fascination with the idea of an art referring only to itself.

All the same, the muted melancholy of the light bulb's isolation and deadness points towards a wider purpose. Floyer's sad little room-fixture would not look wholly out of place in a photograph by Jane and Louise Wilson. When a hand pretends to pull a finger off another hand in her *Untitled*, 1995 video, violence enters her work in the guise of harmless game-playing. Perhaps there is a sexual inference in the image as well, but Floyer does not bring an erotic dimension to the forefront of her work.

Hermione Wiltshire, by contrast, is alive to sensuality in everything she produces. When she uses finger imagery, in a photographic piece called *My Touch*, 1993 (cat. 82), tactile feelings are aroused at once. The glass covering the photograph of a fingerprint magnifies the image to the point where every line and crease is revealed with the clarity of a police investigation. If she seems close in this respect to Borland's forensic concerns, Wiltshire takes us in a different direction with her

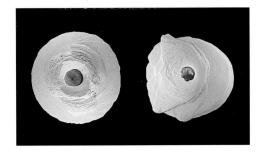

Hermione Wiltshire
83 **Two Points of Speech in Sight**
1993

other work. The photograph of a pursed mouth lodged at the centre of *Two Points of Speech in Sight*, 1993 (cat. 83) has the force of an intimate anatomical disclosure. The plaster surrounding it flows with an organic rhythm, suggesting the soft insides of a body, and the raised glass lens protecting the mouth image seems to be looking back at the spectator.

Wiltshire has long been preoccupied with the idea of undercutting whatever titillating or pornographic potential her images may possess. In one series of framed photographic works, she juxtaposes a mannequin's stockinged leg, or a glowing egg apparently covered in goose-pimples, with banal, *bijou* or hallucinatory objects. She also delights in making the viewer strain to identify the images in her sculpture. As spectators struggle to decide precisely what these forms might represent, they realise that Wiltshire has turned them into avid investigators. The more her sculpture evades recognition, the more intrigued and resolute we become. Even the most chaste gallery-goer becomes aware of the fragile borderline dividing the viewer from the voyeur.

The same uneasy responses are aroused by Wiltshire's *Casanova*, 1995 (cat. 85), a computer-generated image dominating a large screen. When the animated sequence begins, we are confronted with a harmless white dish. Suddenly a golden soufflé emerges, pushing upwards to a prodigious height. There it stands, commanding and erect. But the moment of phallic, self-raising triumph in the kitchen soon passes. The soufflé sinks as rapidly as it ascended, reducing *Casanova*, 1995 from a celebration of domesticated virility to an exposé of humiliating detumescence.

Although teasing comedy plays a part in Wiltshire's work, it is charged with pathos as well. In an ambitious installation originally made for the disused Dreadnought Seamen's Mission Hospital at Greenwich, the floor is apparently splattered with drops of water. They sparkle in the light and gradually disclose the penis photographs within the globules of glass. This time, the image's identity is beyond dispute in every case. But far from celebrating potency, the spilled components of *Seamen*, 1991 look forlorn. Strewn around as if in the aftermath of ejaculation, they seem just as likely to die as Hirst's butterflies and Gallaccio's fast-withering flowers.

The World Outside

Some artists prefer to escape from interior rumination and explore society at large. In her most well-known work, **Gillian Wearing** went out on to the streets, stopped people, asked them to write down on a sheet of paper what they were thinking, and photographed them with the result. The series of pictures grew, over a protracted period, to over four hundred, and they provide an arresting range of insights into British preoccupations during the early 1990s. Some responses, inevitably, are little more than banal, knee-jerk one-liners, but a surprising number of the signs go a great deal further, relaying unexpected and often poignant messages about the way we live now.

Take, for instance, the correctly dressed young man who seems such an epitome of Conservative values. With his neat haircut, apparently smug smile and air of prosperity, he appears to embody the entrepreneurial beliefs of the 1980s. Something has happened to the boom-years philosophy, however. Recession, along with the paralysis and privation it often precipitated, shouts from the capital letters scrawled across his sheet like graffiti on a street wall: I'M DESPERATE.

The disparity between the words and their writers' facial expressions gives many of the photographs their bite. QUEER + HAPPY runs one blithe message, held up in apparent triumph next to the man's head. But his features are marked by tension and the ruefulness in his grin suggests a far more embattled outlook.

A whole gamut of possible replies is encompassed in *Signs . . .*, 1992/93 (cat. 74), from the cheerful defiance of the three tipsy siblings who declare ME AND MY BROTHERS SAY BOLLOCKS, to the stubbly young man in spectacles with his contemplative observation EVERYTHING IS CONNECTED IN LIFE THE POINT

Gillian Wearing
Still from

76 **Confess all on video. Don't worry you will be in disguise. Intrigued? Call Gillian . . .** 1994

IS TO KNOW IT AND UNDERSTAND IT. But the fundamental note, beneath all the banter and street philosophy, centres on a sense of rootless anxiety. Debilitating hardship and the lack of a home continually surface, amounting to a cumulative indictment of deep social fissures. Scant prospect of relief can be detected in messages which often end as a cry from the heart: I HAVE BEEN CERTIFIED AS MILDLY INSANE, or COME BACK MARY LOVE YOU GET BACK MARY.

The frankness of the responses is often astonishing and would not have been achieved by an artist armed with an alienating questionnaire. Wearing's approach was as open as possible. She thrives on collaboration, even to the point where she photographs herself in bed with transsexuals. Establishing her own identity alongside those who have decided to change their sex, Wearing holds the camera release button as if to assure the viewer that no unseen voyeur is manipulating the image. A similar desire to guard against exploitation typifies a project that started with an advertisement in *Time Out* magazine: 'Confess all on video. Don't worry you will be in disguise. Intrigued? Call Gillian.' The outcome, at once ridiculous and painfully disconcerting, is perhaps the most bizarre manifestation of Wearing's determination to carry on from where Mass-Observation* left off, and testifies to the private concerns of a notoriously secretive nation.

Mark Wallinger is also driven by a consuming curiosity about his native country. But he darts from photography and video to painting, and constantly views the present through the perspective of history. Recently, his work has focused on the quintessentially English obsession with equestrian matters. Entering his last one-person show was like walking into a top trainer's stable. Impeccably groomed thoroughbreds were lined up on the white walls. Painted with smoothness and precision, these polished images seemed custom-designed to hang near eighteenth-century racers by George Stubbs.

But then their meaning changes. For these cool, well-mannered pictures turn

* Mass-Observation was a project started in the 1930s involving anthropologists, writers, artists, photographers and a workforce of untrained volunteers, all of whom compiled information on modern British life and culture – especially the working class.

out, in every case, to depict a divided animal. The front and rear halves come from different stallions and Wallinger makes no attempt to hide the disjunction. Although they share the same maternal bloodline, these frankly disparate parts are brought into an unsettling union. Another artist might easily have made them grotesque. To Wallinger's credit, however, these paintings never jar. They retain a streamlined elegance worthy of high-class mounts, and this seductive emphasis on pedigree makes the fault-line running through each canvas even more subversive. If Wallinger did not genuinely savour the gleaming strength of racehorses, his desire to question their origin and purpose could have resulted in heavy-handed work. As it is, the stallion paintings are subtly ambiguous, poised half-way between celebration and scepticism.

Wallinger's attitude to the painting tradition is just as hard to pin down. Fascinated by the eighteenth century, he has no hesitation in seeing himself as an inheritor of Hogarthian social satire. But he is determined to avoid concentrating, in an antiquarian way, on the media William Hogarth employed. Hence Wallinger's use, on a four-monitor video installation, of television coverage from the royal procession at Ascot. The screens present each day's events as four parallel and smoothly-orchestrated displays of smiling, hand-waving and hat-doffing. Regal

Mark Wallinger
72 **Oh No He's Not, Oh Yes He is** 1995

pedigree is brandished here in a highly theatrical and courtly manner reliant on the excitement of the racecourse.

If the Queen and her family are pure-bred products, like the stallions, the continuation of the lineage is in both cases vitally important. In the relatively sober Ascot work, Wallinger's own views remain subservient to the recording of a hallowed tradition. Elsewhere, though, he allows his instinctive humour to erupt in knockabout style. The subversive *Oh No He's Not, Oh Yes He Is*, 1995 (cat. 72) takes the pantomime horse convention and proposes that mating, of a far naughtier and more surreptitious kind, takes place beneath the innocent costume.

Wallinger's fascination with comedy is at its most overt in his ingenious Tommy Cooper video installation. Here we are confronted by a mirror-image of the screen. We can watch ourselves watching Cooper, as we realise that his familiar routine is being played backwards. Laughter turns to puzzlement and, ultimately, a sense of sadness, as we watch him crack jokes and feverishly try on a manic parade of hats. He seems, in the end, caught up in a ritual as bizarre and preposterous as the royal miming from ceremonial coaches at Ascot. England is replete with these unlikely cross-connections, and Wallinger probes our sense of national identity with a keen eye for its inherent greed, class-conscious codes and high-flown dottiness.

When **Gary Hume** first attracted attention, his target was another English affliction: tastefulness. Although his paintings looked abstract, after closer inspection they turned out to be defiantly dependent on the everyday world. Hume's circles, squares and rectangles were borrowed from the windows and panels found in anonymous swing-doors, the kind that proliferate in airports, restaurants and hospitals. Their closed, impersonal surfaces were as disquieting, in an undemonstrative way, as Yass's overtly eerie photographs of hospital corridors.

Hume, however, came to feel confined by his starting-point and worried, too, that a fascination with the psychology of colour was leading him into a cul-de-sac. The prospect of becoming an abstract geometric painter made him restless, so he determined to seek out a far broader range of subjects drawn from the world beyond those doors. Feeding off newspapers and magazines, and to a lesser extent photographs he had taken himself, Hume became overtly engaged with images encompassing at one extreme a fifteenth-century portrait by Petrus Christus and, at the other, a portrait of Tony Blackburn as a three-leaf clover.

The freedom to use anything, from the highest art to the lowest, seems even more important to Hume than to Sam Taylor-Wood. He makes no hierarchical distinctions, and opens up his work still further by employing household paint. Its shiny enamel surface gives Hume's pictures an everyday twist, allying them with a visit to the DIY shop rather than an art gallery. Their reflectiveness offers viewers glimpses of themselves, catching them off-balance, and this edginess extends to the mood of the paintings. The exquisite features of Christus' delicate young woman are almost obliterated by broad swipes of yellow gloss. They are as brusquely applied as the marks in *Funny Girl*, 1995 (cat. 28), where the face is reduced to a pallid mask drained of feeling. Her eyes and lips may be daubed with garish colour, but they only accentuate the feeling of blankness and inertia explored by several other artists in this exhibition.

Gary Hume
27 **Four Feet in the Garden** 1995

Not that Hume generates indifference in the onlooker. He is one of the most inspiriting young painters around and his interest in upsetting the viewer gives his work a consistent attack. In *Baby*, 1995 (cat. 25), his most alarming new painting, the title is inscribed in sprawling, reversed letters across the lower part of the canvas. Their brashness contrasts starkly with the quietness of the dark face above, peering out at us with wide-eyed apprehensiveness. The pathos conveyed here is one of Hume's central concerns, but he is equally capable of irony. In an outstanding recent painting called *Four Feet in the Garden*, 1995 (cat. 27), two pairs of bare feet, pale purple on a dark ground, confront two other pairs. Their toes nearly touch and the expectancy is laced with erotic anticipation. But Hume slyly counters the sensuality with a sense of awkwardness. These feet could well belong to embarrassed English nudists, nervously exposing themselves on a suburban lawn summarised with a few nonchalant strokes of green. Sensual relish is modified, here, by native inhibition and the result could hardly be more richly ambiguous.

Like Hume, **Mat Collishaw** works with intuition rather than a preconceived plan. He also shares the ambition to take the widest possible view, embracing subjects that might seem mutually exclusive but end up, in his work, making unexpected and nourishing connections with each other. A few years ago, he was preoccupied with images of suicide, rape and pornography. Now, however, the vision has broadened and violence is implied rather than placed in the foreground of his art. Collishaw likens himself to a detective and, in that respect, he pieces together fragments of evidence as zealously as Borland. But instead of focusing on the idea of crime and policing, he keeps himself open to the most incongruous experiences imaginable. If Wearing finds stimulus out on the street, so does Collishaw. Far from collaborating with pedestrians, though, he keeps his own counsel and channels heterogeneous observations into his work.

Snowstorm, 1994 (cat. 7), a video projection on a sheet of frosted glass, arose from Collishaw's attempt to deal with the apparently irreconcilable experiences gathered during a walk along Oxford Street. On one side, homeless figures lie in doorways and arouse our compassion. On the other, we find ourselves diverted by the silliness of a fur toy in a magic box. Emotional manipulation is so prevalent, and pulls us in such contrary directions, that we are in danger of succumbing to permanent numbness. *Snowstorm*, 1994 reflects this malaise by presenting an image of a plastic bubble seemingly filled with a kitsch Christmas scene. Picturesque flakes of snow tumble, accompanied by an appropriate Yuletide tune. But all this saccharine fantasy turns sour with the realisation that a homeless sleeper sprawls on the snow-covered ground. As pedestrians walk past unmoved, he turns and cannot settle. The music tinkles remorselessly on and the flakes continue to swirl, oblivious of the figure's predicament.

Rather than remaining an agent of enchantment, the bubble grows oppressive. It traps the anonymous occupant like a prisoner in a cell. The same feeling of restriction sours Collishaw's images of budgies in a cage. They may look attractive but their existence is rigidly circumscribed. Collishaw's delight in playing Floyer-like tricks with illusionism serves only to intensify the perverse mood. Knowing how to charm the spectator with alluring spectacles, each one conjured with the intricacy of a miniaturist, Collishaw nevertheless ensures that his entertainments are informed by fear, nausea and helplessness in the face of potential chaos.

The Legacy of Childhood

The imperatives governing an artist's imagination can often be affected by concerns developed in early life, and hints of such influences are detectable in some of the works already discussed. To a certain extent, Jane and Louise Wilson may owe their fascination with interior worlds to formative memories of the room they shared as children. Collishaw's interest in musical toys suggests a similar debt to childhood, and Roberts' concentration on medical appliances seems informed by the anxiety a young child might feel when confronted with equipment in a dental surgery.

Such experiences can linger in the artist's mind with surprising force but, in **Kerry Stewart**'s work, the legacy of childhood assumes a far greater significance. It has shaped much of her sculpture since 1993, when she placed a fibreglass charity figure of a cripple in a work called *The Boy from the Chemist is Here to See You*, 1993. Barely visible behind a semi-opaque glass door, the boy evokes memories of dusty shop-fronts where donation-box figures waited plaintively for coins to be pressed through their head-slots. But Stewart implies that the sculpture has somehow returned from the past, miraculously mobile and ready to disrupt our privacy with his uncomfortable, nagging presence.

However mute and defenceless her figures may be, they are stiffened by a curious spirit of obstinacy as well. The boy insists on hovering at the door, like a menacing toy sprung to life in a nightmare. A similar painted figure of a pregnant schoolgirl stands her ground stubbornly, even though her ripening stomach already threatens to burst through her drab institutional pullover. Whatever embarrassment she may feel is countered by an innate sense of resolve, like the twins in a more recent sculpture who stare, stunned yet upright, as if marooned in a friendless school playground.

Stewart herself knows what it is like to feel displaced and alien. Moving from her native Scotland to England at the age of thirteen, she found herself shunned and lonely. But there is no self-pity in the work she produces with such single-minded deliberation. A strong vein of humour informs *Ghost*, 1995, a collaboration with Ana Genoves, in which a large polystyrene phantom brandishes its bed-sheet wrapping with shameless gusto. This is the ultimate spectre of nocturnal childhood anxiety and yet rendered with so much comic-book élan that hilarity breaks through.

All the same, the pathos in Stewart's disarmingly direct art is real enough. The image of a drowned dog, made for a lakeside location in a park, is calculated to puncture the idyll of its pastoral setting. So is the vomiting man in period costume and the neon sign ironically announcing at the entrance to an empty path that there will be a PARTY HERE TONIGHT. Coldness runs through Stewart's work, guaranteeing its freedom from sentimentality, but it is matched by robust emotion. Her figures nag at the conscience in a deliberately naive yet independent way, asserting that the discarded realm of childhood will never go away.

Georgina Starr has no intention of letting it disappear. In a complex new work called *Visit to a Small Planet*, 1995 (cat. 58), she uses as her springboard an old Jerry Lewis movie of the same name. According to a childhood memory, she had experienced it as a hugely funny and inventive film about a man from outer space equipped with formidable powers. For six months Starr tried to locate the movie, but all she discovered was the exact time on a Saturday morning in 1978 when the television in her home transmitted it. Although only ten at the time, she still vividly recalls watching the film and reacting to the family life around her: Starr's parents arguing excitedly, while she gobbled ravioli from a tin and devoured TV programmes with equal enthusiasm. So she decided to make the work without seeing the film itself, relying instead on recollection and the ravioli's ability to conjure, like an updated supermarket equivalent of Proust's madeleine, the fantasies she harboured during that distant period.

The ten-year-old Starr was enthralled by Jerry Lewis's ability to don a glowing orange helmet and read people's minds, converse with animals and make himself invisible. She used to imagine herself enacting the same miracles, to the accompaniment of Dean Martin's cloying songs on the film's soundtrack. Starr, who attaches more importance to words than most artists, wrote an elaborate script based on these recollections. The video pieces she went on to produce all centre on the helmeted artist eating ravioli, having Lewis-like conversations with a cat, experimenting with mind-reading and trying to make herself vanish.

Then, at last, she found the original film. It proved deeply disappointing. The brilliant technicolour movie of her memory turned out to be black-and-white. Far from side-splitting, Jerry Lewis now seemed merely irritating. Dean Martin was nowhere to be heard and Lewis did not even wear an orange helmet. Apart from a dance scene, which Starr is now considering for a new work, the film made her wonder why on earth it ever seemed exciting.

The answer must be that Lewis's supernatural powers awoke in the young Starr an overriding desire to transcend human limitations. The fact that she retains such strong recollections of *Visit to a Small Planet* indicates how important those fantasies remain to her today, and how she insists on keeping them alive in her imagination. Perhaps the key to their continuing attraction lies in the sheer unattainability of those feats. Even as a child, Starr must have known that they were impossible. But they remain potent, partly because she has always been shy and finds immense satisfaction in anything that promises to conquer diffidence. Ultimately, though, the experience of watching her quirky videos in their darkened cubicles must testify to a wider impulse on Starr's part. Dissatisfied with the shortcomings of life in the 1990s, like so many artists of her generation, she ends up combating despondency with an act of defiant celebration.

Permindar Kaur
29 **Innocence** 1993

Remembrance of childhood likewise fuels the art of **Permindar Kaur**, but these recollections have the capacity to haunt it as well. Her finest work seems to have been made by a woman who ruminates, time and again, on the insecurities in a child's mind. The objects she produces often resemble toys and they are notable for their vulnerability. There is nothing playful about them. Rather do they appear ominous, as if gifted with the power to foresee the future. In *Untitled*, 1995 (cat. 33), a costume made of green fabric dangles from the wall. Its legs terminate in copper boots, while an equally burnished crown beaten from the same material caps the head. But the costume remains empty. Loose folds run down its surface and the owner's absence seems fateful. Although it could simply be an item in a child's dressing-up cupboard, this inert form also says something about the ultimate futility of an adult's lust for aggrandisement.

Exploring Kaur's work is akin to moving through the rooms of an uncannily deserted house. In *Untitled*, 1993 (cat. 30), two piles of garments are deposited, with conspicuous neatness, on the end of a bed. Despite their crisp contours and fresh colours, they seem to have been abandoned. The bed itself is stark and shorn of anything that would guarantee comfort. The shadows cast by its straps on the floor beneath reinforce their resemblance to the bars of a cage. This could easily be the rudimentary furniture in a cell, or perhaps the bed associated with a culture radically removed from our own.

Conscious of her Indian and British background, Kaur aims at exposing national barriers along with the contradictions inherent in cultural fragmentation. In *Cot*, 1994 (cat. 31), the brilliant red fabric seems inviting at first. But then we begin to wonder why the cot has been filled almost to the point of congestion, and its sides take on a defensive appearance. They seem bent on shutting the rest of the world out, as well as preparing the child who inhabits the cot for a life governed by a siege mentality.

Perhaps the most concise and poignant of all these works is the ironically entitled *Innocence*, 1993 (cat. 29). Flattened for display purposes, like an exhibit in a costume museum, the little girl's dress nevertheless retains a certain flamboyance. Still, whatever childish appeal it may possess is compromised by the iron dagger slung from the front. For the time being, the weapon is dormant in a scabbard. But its prominence ensures ease of access, suggesting that the garment's owner must be ready at any moment to clasp the dagger and fight for her survival.

No such open aggression is discernible in **Jordan Baseman**'s work, with its emphasis on the gentle flow of human hair. The longer we scrutinise his art, though, the less harmless it becomes. The shirt in *Closer to the Heart*, 1994 could easily have been worn by one of the twin boys in Stewart's *Untitled*, 1995, and this ordinary white button-down garment exudes a similar feeling of repression. Even so, Baseman makes sure that the shirt's mimicking of adult conformity is undermined by the rush of dark hair, sprouting so surprisingly from the top of the left arm. It descends a long way below the cuff, formidable enough in its profusion to tilt the entire shirt down on one side. The hair seems to be dragging the garment , and by implication its wearer, towards a level of experience alarmingly removed from the uniformity imposed on children.

The hair itself is not manufactured. Baseman acquires it from a wholesale supplier to wigmakers and the reality of these strands adds considerably to his work's discomforting presence. The strands cascade from the arm of the boy's shirt as if he had been assailed by the sudden, grotesque onset of uncontrolled puberty. It has an unbalancing effect presumably because the uniformity symbolised by the shirt has done nothing to prepare its owner for adolescence at its most rampant. Baseman believes that western society tries hard to disguise and deny the animal side of our nature, leaving us feeling hopeless and fearful when we fail to conform. Hence the melancholy inherent in the tumbling hair, which engulfs the garment in its mournful downward plunge.

No one escapes from these tendrils, each threaded so painstakingly through the material Baseman employs. In *Manifest Destiny*, 1995 (cat. 1) they thrust out of a baby's bib, besmirching its purity with a beard-like mass of strands. They stir at the merest breath and assert themselves on all twenty-six of the shirts hanging from a wide rack in *Words Will Never Hurt Me*, 1995 (cat. 4). Here they grow, in each case, from a letter of the alphabet sewn on the garment near the heart. This time, the shirts appear to be intended for adolescents, but the slight increase in size only makes their stillness all the more ominous. They look paralysed, unable to cope

Jordan Baseman
1 **Manifest Destiny**
1995

with the overwhelming growths; and their inertia seems eerily close to death. Human hair, after all, has a habit of continuing to grow on corpses. So Baseman's becalmed row of garments ends up confronting their prospective wearers with the unavoidable fact of mortality.

Fractured Narratives

In the final analysis, though, many of these artists deliberately present fragmented work, resisting the ever-present desire on our part to impose definitive, settled meanings. In *The Waste Land*, T.S. Eliot's narrator displays a similar reluctance, declaring that:

> You cannot say, or guess, for you know only
> A heap of broken images, where the sun beats,
> And the dead tree gives no shelter, the cricket no relief,
> And the dry stone no sound of water.

Lucia Nogueira's loose assemblages explore a sense of fracture strikingly in sympathy with Eliot's lines. Her images are broken because she cannot imagine working in any other way. Brazilian-born but resident in England for nearly twenty years, she feels forever caught between two cultures and unable to make their disparate identities cohere. Instead of regarding her consciousness of being foreign as a weakness, however, she has learned in recent years how to mine it as a source of strength.

Lucia Nogueira
39 **Pinocchio** 1995

Nogueira makes a virtue out of incompleteness. She is instinctively drawn to the fissures that occur when one line in your life is severed, leaving no clear link with an alternative. Her exhibition at the Ikon Gallery in Birmingham and at Camden Arts Centre in London in 1994 was alive with particles and loose ends, brought together in an arena where sundering rather than unity became the norm. An old child's tricycle sprawled on the floor, separated from its front wheel as if in the wake of an accident. Thin rubber piping ran through both fragments but not as connecting threads. In each case, it stopped short of joining another element, and nearby a far longer stretch of piping spilled pointlessly from a low-slung tubular barrier. Although attempts had been made to tie the components together, linking the upended sink with the crocodile clip and a piece of glass tubing, they all remained isolated and incomplete.

The juxtaposition of these ordinary objects, which prove that Nogueira can make stimulating art out of anything, is nevertheless eloquent in itself. Diverse and broken they may be, but they are not irreconcilable. In their fragmentation lies a kind of stammering truth. Even when an object as complete as a chandelier is presented, it seems only a part of a larger narrative otherwise beyond our grasp. Elusiveness is central to Nogueira's vision. Like the balls forever erupting, bouncing and disappearing in her new, room-size work, everything appears to be in a perpetual state of transition, at once cruelly tantalising and pregnant with multiple possibilities.

Tacita Dean would understand why Nogueira's art remains fundamentally lacking in certainties. In common with Borland and Collishaw, she sees herself as an amateur sleuth who follows a trail of clues and amasses evidence. However possessed she may become during the chase, though, the pursued story never quite fits together. It remains laughably incomplete, and this absurdity is enlivened by a spirit of wild delight.

The quixotic oddity of the assignments Dean sets herself does not prevent her from relaying her findings in a sober, authoritative style. After devoting her first film to the tale of a woman searching for beards in different countries, she then turned her attention to the *Martyrdom of St Agatha (in several parts)*, 1994 (cat. 10). The voice on the film's soundtrack is quiet, almost professorial, describing with dignity how the devout Agatha of Catania refused the lecherous advances of the Roman Consular Quintian. The camera tracks across her native Sicily, searching for traces of the third-century woman who became a legend after Quintian cut off her breasts.

The severed mammaries are Agatha's most abiding memorial, echoed in the shape of objects as disparate as church bells and volcanoes. Even more bizarre is the saint's 'fiery crotch', emblem of her 'flaming virginity' which, according to Dean's narrative, proved 'too hot for the relic hunters to handle'. But the most remarkable sequence in the film is a hushed ritual, revolving around the solemn preparation by nuns of facsimile breasts. The reverence with which these ridiculous yet strangely touching orbs are handed round the table sums up the curious blend, in Dean's film, of wit and questing intensity.

Whatever eroticism and violence can be found in the *Martyrdom of St Agatha (in several parts)*, 1994 is tempered by understatement. The same approach characterises the even more sober *Girl Stowaway*, 1995 (cat. 11), although film here plays a smaller role in a work which also relies on newspaper cuttings, photographs and the dubbing sheets from a British feature film apparently prepared in 1928. Challenging us to separate fiction from fact, Dean tells the labyrinthine story of an Australian stowaway's adventures on board a tall ship called *Herzogin Cecilie*. Voyaging from Port Lincoln to Falmouth, her escapade could have formed the basis of a straightforward linear narrative, but Dean adopts a far more wayward and idiosyncratic approach, blurring the boundaries between documentary and fantasy at will. The curiously androgynous stowaway, Jean Jeinnie, is confused at one stage with Jean Genet; while Dean's attempt to film the wreck of the ship in Starehole Bay is thrown off-course by a young woman's murder on the cliff path. Dean teases us with coincidence and enigma throughout *Girl Stowaway*, 1995, making no more of a bid than Nogueira to fill in the missing fragments and arrive at a neatly resolved state of wholeness.

Since **Chris Ofili** is committed to painting, and strives for an openly emotional art without 'too much head-work going on', the fracturing in his work occurs within the context of a canvas. It is no less disruptive, however, and even carries the power to affront. By applying dried gobbets of elephant dung to the picture-surface, he effectively demolishes the prospect of contenting himself with a bland, complacent image. The brute fact of the excrement, collected by the artist from fresh droppings at the zoo, can deliver a blow to the sensibilities of anyone absorbed in the intricacies of Ofili's pigment.

He discovered dung's potential on a visit to Zimbabwe in 1992. Ofili was twenty-four, and in the middle of his MA course at the Royal College of Art. The trip to Africa, where his parents had lived before they settled in Manchester, made him dissatisfied with the acrylic abstractions he was producing. They no longer reflected the intensity of his experience and so he slapped some elephant dung on to an orderly, decorative painting. It was a crude gesture at that stage, but Ofili felt gratified that he had stuck something African on to his otherwise westernised work.

Viewed in retrospect, the Zimbabwe sojourn can be seen to have dramatically revitalised his art. A trip to an ancient cave, where one wall was festooned with red, yellow and blue dots, awoke him to a form of mark-making utterly removed from his previous brushwork. Ofili also realised that African healers used baboon dung as a natural ingredient in their medicine. He began to play with beads, planting them in the elephant dung where they glittered like coloured map-pins. He poured resin on his pictures, too, vying with the pools created by elephants

Chris Ofili
43 **Bag of Shit** 1995

when they irrigate their newly-dumped excrement with urine.

All the same, Ofili has no desire to make a wholly rebarbative art. He is fired by the ambition to redefine the tired idea of beauty, and to that end spends months over highly-wrought, jewel-like paintings which shimmer with their rich accumulation of layers. The dung still plays an indispensable part, interrupting the pictures and ensuring that they never become too seductive. But he sees the conflict between shit and pigment as a friendly argument.

It is a risky strategy: an application of dung could easily ruin the painting he has laboured over for several months. Even so, he considers it an essential foil to the visionary, Blake-like ardency of his current work. The pictures all rest on dung supports, rather than hanging conventionally on walls. Leaning out into the viewer's space, they take on an almost sculptural presence. Ofili confirms the affection he feels for the elephants by naming many of his pictures, like *Rara & Mala*, 1994 (cat. 42), after the obliging animals who supply him with the substance that gives his art so much of its dark, provocative tension.

If Ofili discovered his own direction by introducing 'foreign' elements to painting, **Steve McQueen** explores his fragmented preoccupations as a young black artist through the medium of film. His work recently appeared in an international exhibition at the Institute of Contemporary Arts called *Mirage: Enigmas of Race, Difference and Desire*. The show took its cue from the writings of the Martinique-born Frantz Fanon whose book, *Black Skin, White Masks*, 1952, proved a widely influential study of colonialism and its traumatic psychological legacy. Like Fanon, McQueen refuses to accept stereotyped attitudes. 'Look, a Negro! . . . Mama, see the Negro! I'm frightened!' wrote Fanon, dissecting the insidious blend of voyeurism and terror which so often fanned colonial prejudice. McQueen's *Bear*, 1993 (cat. 34) plays with the notion of a threatening black aggressor, but soon replaces it with a far more stimulating alternative.

Slowly, almost languorously, the camera moves in searching close-up across a black man's face. Then it cuts to another black face, plumper and more anxious. He rubs sweat from his lips, moving nervously from side to side as if limbering up for a fight. But the promised struggle between the two men never really takes place. Both naked, they grin at each other. They even embrace. When eventually their bodies lock in a bout of wrestling, it soon gives way to a slow-motion, lyrical dance.

Time and again the camera lingers on the faces of the two men, inviting viewers to question their own expectations about how the encounter might develop. Rather than serving up a predictable stew of macho violence, McQueen turns the supposed combat on its head. A teasing vein of tenderness and affection runs through the film, tantalising us with ambiguities. By staying close to both bodies, encircling them with shadow and selecting dramatic camera angles, *Bear*, 1993 sustains the aura of mystery throughout. The final dance, as well as banishing all thoughts of war between the two men, seems to rejoice in the film's escape from racial clichés.

Still, there is nothing complacent about McQueen's vision. His next film, *Five Easy Pieces*, 1995 (cat. 35), begins with an image of unease: a tightrope, viewed in arresting close-up, is flung across the screen and hangs there like a challenge. Sure enough, a foot begins to move across it, but the possibility of danger recedes once the precision of the tightrope-walker's tread has been established. McQueen then cuts to an aerial shot of hula-hooping men. It is at once elegant and dynamic. Figures and hoops both cast shadows on the ground, making up a composition as poised as the aerial vantages explored by Alexander Rodchenko and other Russian artists in the post-Revolutionary period.

But there is tension here, along with a veiled sense of erotic defiance. One hula-hooper is seen from below, his body caught in provocative gyrations. Then a man in white shorts is seen from a similar vantage, standing expectantly with legs apart. A few seconds later, a woman in a sequinned top starts moving up and down. She might be the tightrope-walker, but McQueen's fragmentary style leaves us feeling uncertain. Only the walker's shoes are shown, making their way across the diagonal rope. The camera is now directly below, involving us vividly in sensations of danger. When the man in shorts begins to urinate, apparently straight down on us, the apprehensive mood grows.

Not for long, though. Water bubbles fill the screen, forming patterns as appealing in their way as the hula-hoop circles. McQueen leaves the camera on them as they slowly burst, and the hint of melancholy is confirmed by a final shot of the hula-hoopers themselves. Their gyrations come to an end, leaving us with a sense of exhaustion and aimlessness. The incessant mood-shifts in *Five Easy Pieces*, 1995 (cat. 35) vary as much as the camera angles, and they add up to an experience riddled with ambiguities.

By a coincidence, a tightrope also appeared in **Douglas Gordon**'s first London one-person show, at the Lisson Gallery in 1995. But in this case it was real and the steel cable divided one room in an almost territorial way. Stretching in a taut diagonal across the space, this high-tension practice wire seemed both expectant and inviting. But a large colour photograph on the wall offered a prospect of Niagara Falls, half-obscured by spray. It carried a reminder of the risks which high-wire walking can involve, especially when the emptiness beneath the cable is deep enough to bring on an attack of vertigo.

A spare and rigorous artist, Gordon would never want to present his tightrope in nightmarish terms. But there was still a link between this matter-of-fact installation and the main exhibit in the next room. Here, propped with deceptive casualness against a black pole in the middle of the darkened space, leant a screen. It was the focus of a video projection, and the jerky images flickering there clearly derived from a silent film produced long before Gordon himself was born.

No attempt has been made to hide the ragged, blotchy grain of the original film-stock in $10ms^{-1}$, 1994 (cat. 18). It reinforces the desolate mood conveyed, in the opening seconds, by the room where the action takes place. Apart from an iron-frame bed, redolent of a hospital or army barracks, the room is empty and devoid of decoration. But to start with, at least, a pair of naked legs occupies the centre of the screen. They move backwards, forwards and then stop. The camera reveals the whole figure, of a young man who looks sturdy and agile enough to have recovered from whatever ailment he once suffered. No sign of a wound or injury can be detected on his pale body.

Just as we are about to conclude that he is fit to leave, the man suddenly falls over. It happens so fast that the unseen camera operator is also caught off-guard. The figure falls partially out of sight, to the left. He is still lying there when the camera catches up with him. The man tries sitting up, only to fall back sharply on the floor. Then his head moves from side to side, as if to reassure himself that he can still perform a simple feat. By this time, however, a sense of paralysis afflicts the prone form. Well-muscled, he is nevertheless quite unable to make his limbs respond in a normal way.

It is, in one sense, a gruelling film to watch. Whatever distress we may feel, though, is compounded by an awareness of absurdity. As the figure's movements become more manic, so he sheds some of his humanity and begins to resemble a dummy. Lacking the strings that might restore co-ordination, the hapless puppet is reduced to a permanent state of oscillation between striving and collapse. He comes to seem merely frantic, a mannequin well-proportioned enough for a shop-window who has, inexplicably, spun out of control.

The fact that the camera lingers on him in such a deadpan, methodical way fosters a voyeuristic mood. The filming has clearly been carried out for medical purposes, and the knowledge that the young man's torment is real only adds to the vicarious fascination. Gordon has edited and manipulated the footage for his own ends, doubtless heightening the patient's air of futility. He must want us to become engrossed in the mortification of the figure's strivings and, as we do so, feel guilty about the perverse satisfaction involved in watching the man's pathetic manoeuvres so closely.

The guilt is compounded when we realise that the falling man was a victim of the First World War. The incessant need to avoid hostile fire, whether in the trenches or out on exposed land leading to the enemy's lines, might have made him succumb to a chronic urge to stay on the ground. However much he may wish to stand up, the pain of accumulated memories forces his legs to surrender their strength. They stubbornly refuse to let go of the past. The writhing, toppling figure seems trapped in a repeating film-loop which always ends with his horizontal, twitching body and then, remorselessly, starts all over again. Injury time, in sporting parlance, has a finite span. But here, in an art-work that brings a distant trauma to bear on our own thwarted condition in the 1990s, the damage seems set to last for ever.

Like all the other artists in this exhibition, Gordon repudiates facile optimism. They grew up, increasingly disenchanted, in the century's declining years and found it wanting. Unencumbered by any threadbare idealism, and spurning the visionary fervour which gave so many earlier avant-garde artists a headlong impetus, they thrive instead on a bracing diet of irony and scepticism. In certain quarters, it has earned them a great deal of vilification – especially in Britain, where a knee-jerk condemnation of challenging new art has for long been notoriously endemic. Alone among the great capitals of Europe, London still clings to the folly of denying itself a fully-fledged museum of modern art. The present century will be over by the time the Tate Gallery's new Bankside building opens, in a belated acknowledgement that the work of our era deserves to be viewed extensively and in its own right.

But at least our inexcusable tardiness is redeemed by the artists we produce. Refusing to be hampered by this home-grown mistrust of the modern, they have made emergent British art into a focus of international attention. Their preoccupation with injury in its widest sense, and the death of old illusions, is readily understood across Europe. So, too, is their lack of overriding faith in any foreseeable amelioration. All they adhere to is an obstinate belief in their ability, as artists, to assert the rights of the independent imagination and never settle for a spurious sense of reassurance. There is nothing cosy about the new British art. It finds more occasion for melancholy than celebration. Even so, the danger of lapsing into *fin de siècle* despair is countered by a defiant, and thoroughly paradoxical, spirit of tough-minded exuberance.

Plates

Jordan Baseman

3 **Shoes (Size 8)** 1995

4 **Words Will Never Hurt Me** 1995

Christine Borland

5 **Black Museum** 1994
Installation at Kröller-Muller Museum

Mat Collishaw

7 Still from **Snowstorm** 1994

Tacita Dean

10 Still from **Martyrdom of St Agatha (in several parts)** 1994

By evening, the Duchess gave up, her back was broken.

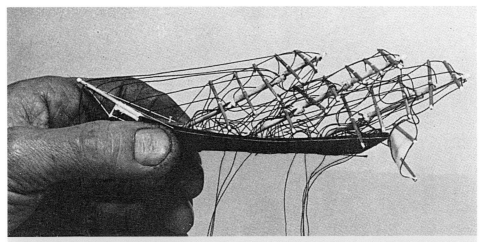

Those with any experience knew the Duchess was dying.

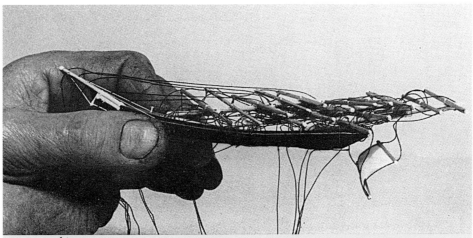

Her proud masts came tumbling down to lay in the sea beside her, and she disappeared over night.

Ceal Floyer

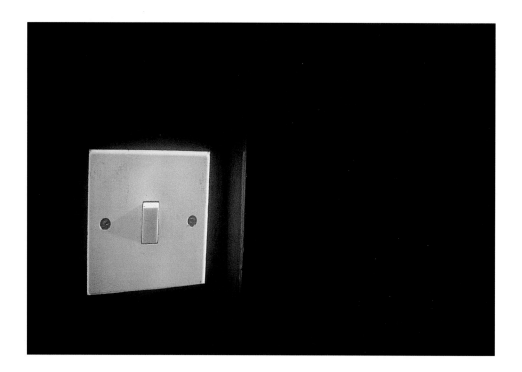

12 **Light Switch** 1992

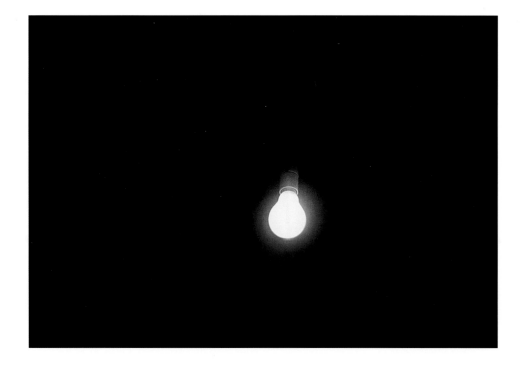

13 **Light** 1994

John Frankland

You Can't Touch This 1993
Laminated polythene and wood
Installation at Hales Gallery, London
Courtesy of Saatchi Collection, London

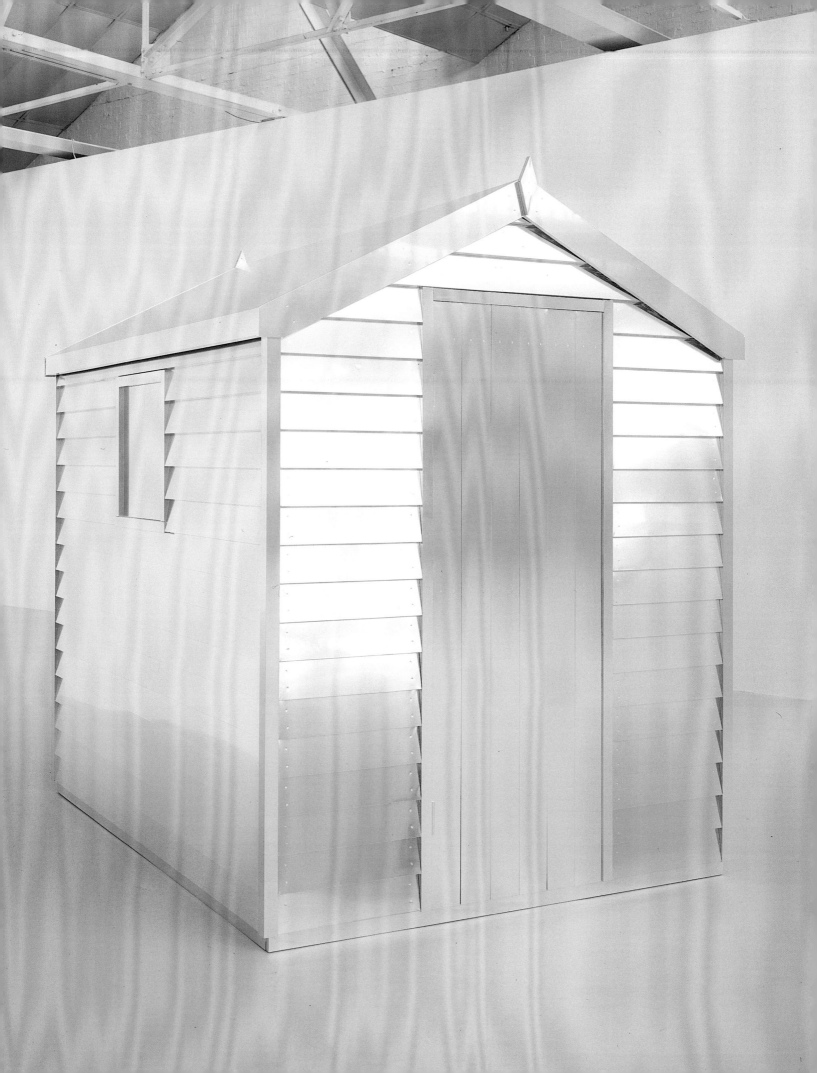

Anya Gallaccio

head over heals 1995
Gerberas
Courtesy of Stephen Friedman Gallery

Couverture 1994
Chocolate installation, Filiale, Basle, July 1994
Courtesy of Roman Kurzmayer, Bottmingen

Douglas Gordon

18 **10ms⁻¹** 1994

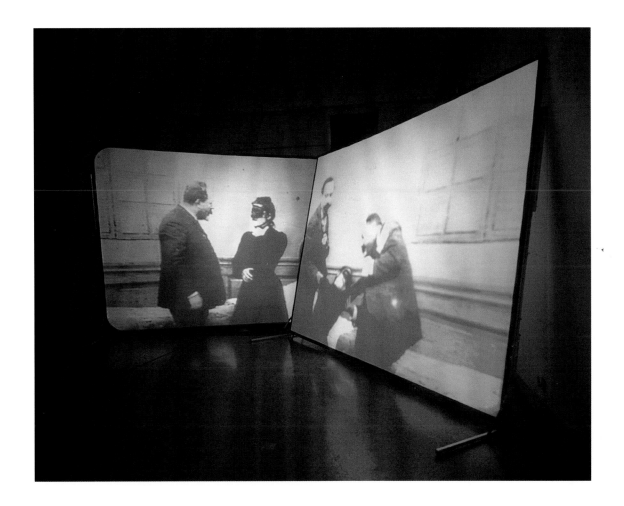

19 **Hysterical** 1995

Damien Hirst

22 **I Feel Love** 1994/95

21 **Away from the Flock** 1994

Gary Hume

25 **Baby** 1995

Permindar Kaur

30 **Untitled** 1993

31 **Cot** 1994

Steve McQueen

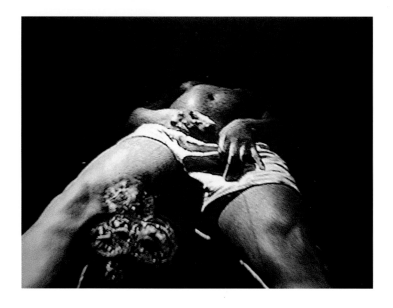

35 Stills from **Five Easy Pieces** 1995

34 **Bear** 1993

Lucia Nogueira

38 **Catch** 1995

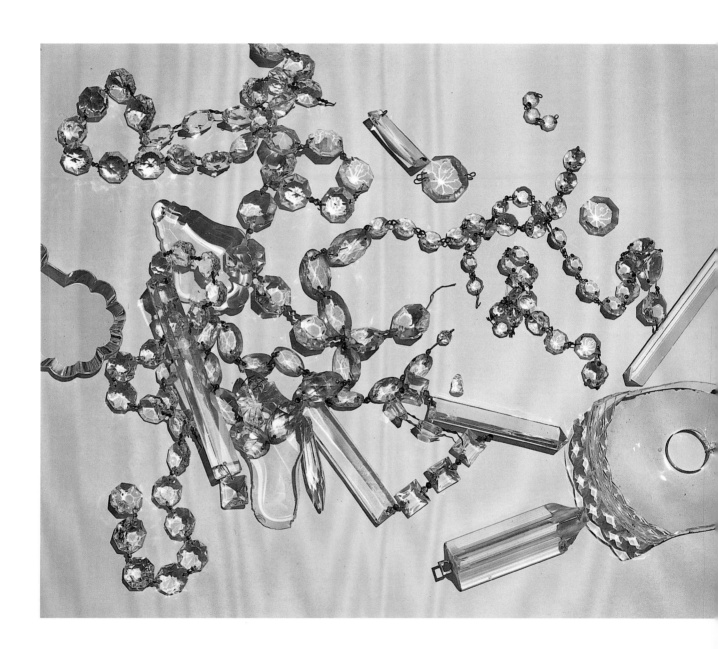

36 **Black** 1994 (detail)

Chris Ofili

41 **Painting with shit on it** 1993

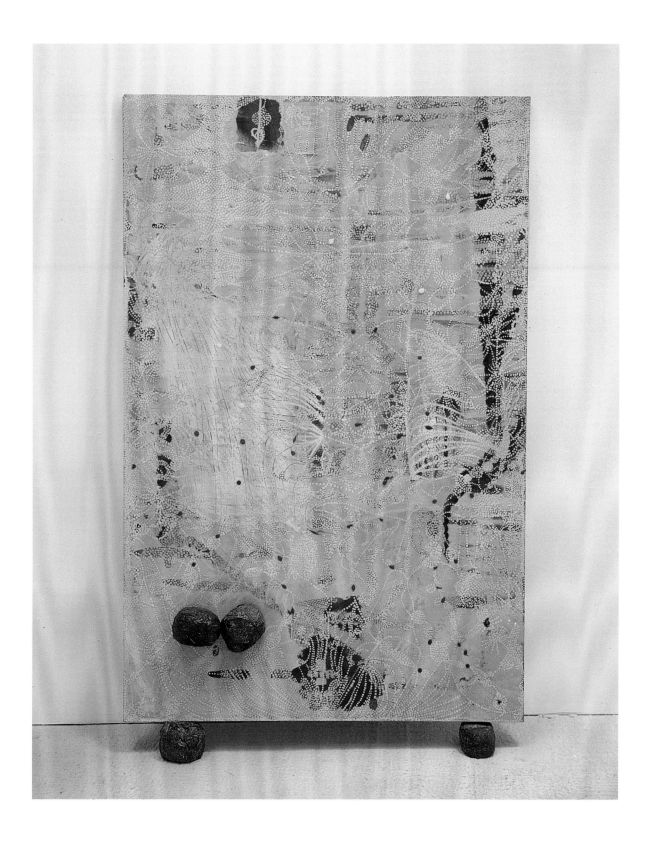

Julie Roberts

46 **Dentist Chair/Leather 19th Century** 1995

49 **Restraining Coat (Female 2)** 1995

Bridget Smith

54 **Empire (Blue)** 1995

56 **Odeon (Green)** 1995

Georgina Starr

58 **Visit to a Small Planet** 1995
(l–r) Stills from **Eating the Ravioli; Cat Conversation;**
How to Make Yourself Invisible; Being Invisible (Blue)

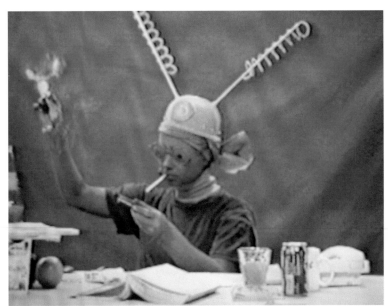

Kerry Stewart

Kerry Stewart (in collaboration with Ana Genoves)
Ghost 1995
Fibreglass
Height: 185.5 cm
Courtesy of Saatchi Collection, London

62 **Party Here Tonight** 1995

Marcus Taylor

Untitled (Single chest freezer) 1992
Clear acrylic sheet
84 x 54 x 54 cm
Courtesy of Jay Jopling, London

65 **Untitled (Model for a Diving Pool 2)** 1994

Sam Taylor-Wood

66 **Killing Time** 1994

Mark Wallinger

68 **Regard a Mere Mad Rager** 1993

71 **Half-Brother (Unfuwain-Nashwan)** 1994/95

Gillian Wearing

75 From **Take Your Top Off** 1993

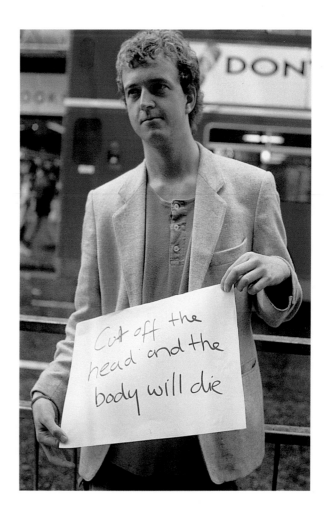

74 From **Signs that say what you want them to say and not signs that say what someone else wants you to say** 1992/93

Jane and Louise Wilson

78 **Hypnotic Suggestion "505"** 1993

Stills from **Crawl Space** 1995
16 mm film / video transfer
Courtesy of the artists

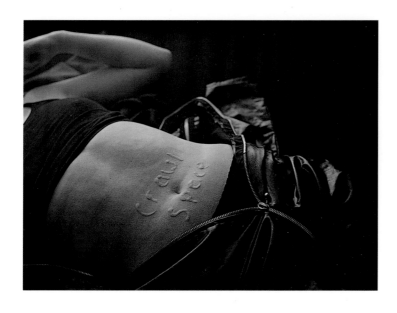

Hermione Wiltshire

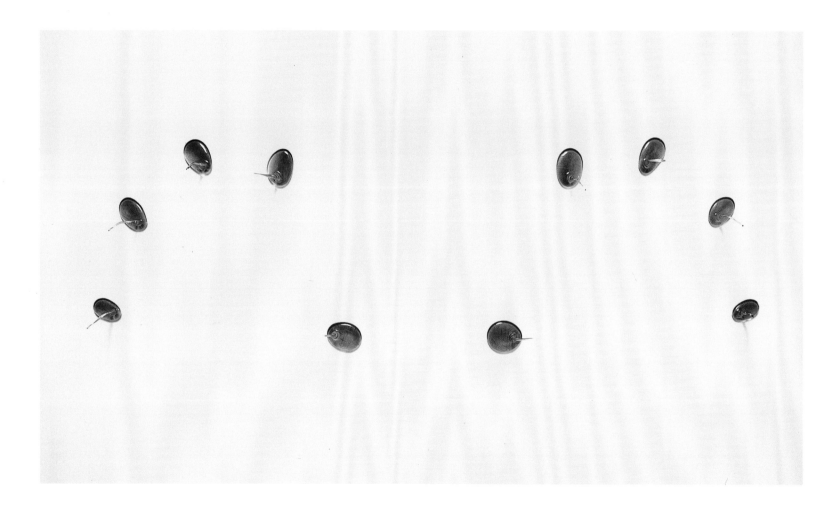

82 **My Touch** 1993
Glass, cibachrome, silicon glue
and aluminium

84 **Seamen II** 1994

Catherine Yass

86 From **Corridors** 1995

ROSE FINN-KELCEY

Questionnaire compiled by Rose Finn-Kelcey
(see inside back cover)

© the contributors, Rose Finn-Kelcey and The South Bank Centre 1995

As an artist co-curating *The British Art Show 4* I felt it was important that my contribution to the catalogue reflect a perspective from 'the other side of the fence'.

The questionnaire format allows concise, insightful information about both the profound and the more mundane aspects of artists' lives and work, behind-the-scenes information not usually associated with the more public task of mediating the work in prose.

Despite pious claims to the contrary, I believe it is interesting to discover how artists think and survive in a climate so frequently hostile to them, where an extra dose of resourcefulness is a pre-requisite for maintaining the unique 'job' that every artist creates for themselves.

The questions are designed to cover a broad range of concerns to elicit the voice of each artist and to allow cross-references from one voice to another. Some of the questions are presumptuous, cheeky even, so I was prepared for a number of blanks. Questionnaires are not orthodox catalogue contributions and for many people likely to have a sting associated with the Press, Social Services and bureaucratic prying.

It seemed appropriate that Richard, Tom and I should also be included as a form of levelling, an antidote to the unavoidable hierarchical position we occupy as selectors.

By implication the questionnaire extends an invitation to artists and to all readers to . . .

Unrelenting Jet Lag and Iron-Hard Jets[11]

Looking back on a year of unrelenting jet lag, a year of monthly trips from Los Angeles to Britain in order to undertake frantic rounds of shows, studios, and meetings; remembering the huge number of slides and videos, the interviews with artists, the lobbying from interested parties, the discussions, the badgering, the wheedling, the pleading; I have to ask, 'What did we accomplish?'

The following essay is an attempt to find an answer. I have written a partial reconstruction, from memory and some notes, of the discussions Richard Cork, Rose Finn-Kelcey and I had as we came to agree on the show, mixed with my understanding of what the show is, and what the art amounts to. This will be a bit of a tale, a rewriting in search of coherence, done in the knowledge that too much coherence is a lie.

I think it would be truthful to begin by saying that we all wanted the exhibition to be ambitious in the sense that it would exercise the public's reception of contemporary art. We did not want to be pointlessly ingratiating, but rather to make our viewers somewhat uncomfortable with their preconceived ideas about art. Above all, we wanted to create an exhibition that would encourage those who saw it to take responsibility for their own ideas about the work, and not accept the artists' views, or ours, or those expressed in the press.

An example of the kind of difficulty I have in mind here can be found in Christine Borland's uncompromising *From Life* which was first shown at Tramway in Glasgow in October 1994[2]. The central matter of this piece is a consideration of how we interpret the clues and signs offered by the material world and how we use this interpretation to make life meaningful. The material clue on offer here is a human skeleton and three Portakabins containing three possible ways of approaching it. The first presents the skeleton itself, packed in a box and placed casually on a folding table. The second functions as a kind of library in which are stored and displayed a range of interpretative tools, from forensic science to TV thrillers. In here we see (on slide and video) the artist at work with teams of scientists, 'medical artists', and other experts. The final Portakabin is set up more like an art gallery and contains a bronze head on a plinth and a short text outlining some characteristics that might define an actual person whose features can be deduced from the skeleton in the box in the first Portakabin. Overall the exhibit has the air of an educational service; you expect to be led around by an earnest guide pointing out the lessons to be learnt. But it is not didactic in that sense. The work is disconcertingly open-ended, insisting in a quiet, non-threatening way that the meaning of the experience has to be constructed by each individual who confronts it. What Borland achieves is a radical questioning of the issue of responsibility in regard to representation. How, and by whom, is a life to be understood?

A similar question animates Georgina Starr's goofy but perceptive investigations of representational orthodoxies. Partial to using complex ways of getting simple results, Starr engineers chance through picturesque acts to get at systems of meaning. She will try to learn about a Dutch writer, for example, not by meeting him or reading his work, but by consulting astrologists, palmreaders, handwriting specialists, and so on. (This comic resort to expert witness recalls Borland's straight-faced use of authorities, but where Borland consults the law, Starr entertains diviners who are away with the fairies.) Starr similarly inverts the conventional organisation of knowledge in her comprehensive work, *Nine Collections of the Seventh Museum*, 1994. This parody of museum practices consists of snapshots, bric-à-brac, and personal objects made and collected by a lonely, self-obsessed girl, all brought together in a photo archive, a poster and a CD Rom that project a relentless cheeriness and sad doggedness at once. The realisation that this museum is a hotel room

1. In an essay on Damien Hirst in *Modern Painters* (Fine Art Journals, London, summer 1994), Will Self claims that William Empson once characterised the typical exhibition catalogue essay as: 'A steady iron-hard jet of absolutely total nonsense'.

2. I discuss a number of works here that proved unavailable for the show. I regret this, but since they were important in giving shape to my thinking before the practicalities of exhibition-making took over, I include them anyway.

and its collections the result of a two week artist's residency reframes the project as both a critique of museum culture and a sly excursion into sexual politics.

This in turn leads to various issues concerning narrative, questions of beginnings and ends, of completeness, of lessons learned, or refused. An example of what I mean can be found in Sam Taylor-Wood's video installation *Killing Time*, 1994 (cat. 66). First exhibited at The Showroom in London in July 1994, this savvy mixture of high fantasy and everyday squalor, myth and its modern descendent, soap, appears quite casual but is actually rigorous in form. From the title onwards, *Killing Time* offers an oscillation between banality and hysteria, between sullen silence and a depravity of possession, such that the viewer is sucked into a vortex of contradictory meanings. Despite its casual, even sloppy, air the piece is precise in a funny and dislocating way as it lays bare the emotional structure of narrative.

By contrast, Tacita Dean's reflections on narrative steeped in feminist theory take on a more serious appearance. *Girl Stowaway*, 1995 (cat. 11), with its intricately woven tale presented as film, storyboard, newsclippings and other images, is a highly complex affair. Here, Dean takes a found story and alters it by using accidental rhyme, the evidence of newspaper archives, the happenstance of everyday events, coincidence and a wilful imagination. This insistent reframing provides an analysis of story-telling that proceeds from the construction of sexual identity to the larger issue of the construction of a history. The viewer is led, charmed by the grace of a tale of adventure on the high seas, to a confrontation with the over-arching authority of the master narrative. The falseness of the unitary voice of interpretation is made clear as Dean opens up the fecund possibilities of multiple and very likely (mis)readings. Again and again as we consider the work in the show, we confront the problem of authorship and the crisis of authentic histories that that problem always provokes. In a sense, these questions can be subsumed into the great question of identity – of the subject, of the context, of the discourse, of art. The one thing these artists show only passing interest in is the question of Britishness.

Yet we selectors felt we had to face up to the imposing title, *The British Art Show 4*, at some point during the process. In fact we objected to the title from the beginning. Exhibitions are so often expected to carry unreasonable metaphysical baggage, offering insight into the human condition and so on. To face up to that and to be expected to take on some responsibility for a notion of Britishness that none of us could identify just seemed too much. From the outset we argued for a shrinking of outside expectations, saying the show could not hope to be a survey of national trends but a selection of what we three could agree was the most challenging work made in Britain during the past five years. Thus we early on gave character to a show we eventually discovered could not be un-named.

Of course any exhibition burdened with such a title may raise questions and hackles in Scotland, Wales and Northern Ireland. This is understandable. Yet it is a mistake to seek a representation of the diversity of lived experience in Britain today by playing some kind of numbers game. Contemporary art is a complex business in which artist/producers attempt to circulate their images and ideas through various international markets. To do this successfully, they need access to distribution systems and to a range of jobs that will allow them to pay the rent without taking away too much time from the studio. London, with its network of galleries, magazines, art schools and other artists, provides this in a way no other city in the country can. So, inevitably, the most ambitious artists gravitate there, at least for the years it takes to establish their careers. This truth is very clearly borne out by a glance at the biographies of the artists in this show. Birthplaces dot the map, not only of this country, but of the globe, and indeed the artists here come from a rich variety of backgrounds. Most began their education near home, and then moved to London to finish their undergraduate education or to pursue a postgraduate degree. An adventurous few chose to work on postgraduate studies in Belfast, Glasgow, or abroad, but I think it would be difficult to draw any useful conclusion about this from their work. All have now developed enviable exhibition histories in London and across Europe.

The title might have diverted us into a statistical analysis of the land. But had we followed this path we would have participated in the worst type of bureaucratic tokenism, mounting a show that only a Heritage Ministry could love. Instead we agreed that what we wanted was an exhibition of artwork that slips across boundaries of all sorts, finding meaning between the gaps of the well known and the expected. The circumstances of this particular exhibition helped here; the multiple sites across three cities almost dictated that the show feature fewer artists than in the past, and allowed each an extended space in which to show a body of work.

In the early months of the selection process, Rose Finn-Kelcey and I spent a day together in London looking at art. We criss-crossed the city, from Waddington's to Chisenhale, looking at the artworks on offer. The British question continued to nag and a special exhibit of Prince Charles' watercolours at Sotheby's was irresistible. Since the National Gallery débâcle Prince Charles has assumed the mantle of spokesperson for traditional taste and value. It was no surprise that his pictures were mostly views of landscapes and houses in Scotland, Wales and other picturesque parts of the world that he and his relations own. What they display is an unthinking allegiance to an order of representation that is still feudal at heart. Mischievously, we did briefly consider including these watercolours in the show, as a way of highlighting the problem of identifying authentic Britishness. We quickly discarded the idea as we realised that what really gave the little pictures their interest, what provided the necessary ironic framework that made them interesting, was the elaborate presentation of insignia and signature repeated over the simple but elegant room dividers that served as their support.

Of course the real crown prince of British art is Damien Hirst and he has achieved that eminence by acting like an American artist. His enthusiastic understanding of the way in which spectacular materials and presentation guarantee the attention of the press has given him the kind of notoriety more usually associated with Andy Warhol, Julian Schnabel or Jeff Koons. More interesting, however, is Hirst's ability to mount an encyclopaedic barrage of metaphor such that the viewer reels from the accumulation of perversity, vulgarity and raw emotion. The suspended rot of flesh in formaldehyde is juxtaposed with large stretched canvases covered only with aimless dots. A vast collection of medical instruments is laid out in massive metal and glass cabinets as if to overwhelm us with a vision of the clinical while, nearby, flies buzz around an enclosed bug zapper. Thousands of exotic butterflies are let loose to live out their span in the gallery, or alternatively an array of preserved ones are rather haphazardly pasted to canvas with bright pastel colours. The effect is both dizzying and dazzling, an undeniable kick in the pants to any expectations of propriety in art. It is also quite clear that Hirst has no interest in analysing the state of Britain or contemporary Britishness.

Mark Wallinger emphatically does. Of all the artists in this show it is Wallinger who places the question of national identity at the very core of his work. He is fascinated by all aspects of the social structure and takes great glee in unmasking the absurd ideologies of power and privilege that seek to keep us all in our rightful places. Using monumentally-scaled paintings treated in a realist manner, documentary-style video footage, video installation using clips pirated from broadcast TV, an actual racehorse, bought and trained to run, he throws together images of thoroughbred racing and royalty in a delirious critique of primogeniture. Here we see pictured the rituals of the stud farm and the results of these rituals; the pure-bred colts with a lineage tracing back to stallions commemorated by George Stubbs and the mechanically smiling, arm-waving, hat-wearing descendants of families portrayed by Joshua Reynolds. But if Wallinger only trained his wit on this reflection of a class-bound world, where race, sex and breeding count for everything, his work would remain social satire. Instead, by cross-pollinating this with images from the music hall tradition, he broadens his scope to include an entire national pathology.

If the pantomime horse is the ridiculous inverse of the stud, Tommy Cooper, in the installation *Regard a Mere Mad Rager*, 1993 (cat. 68), becomes a sadly dysfunctional everyman mimicking the formal public gestures of the monarchy. Here, in the funhouse non-space created by a videotape playing backwards in front of a wall-sized mirror, we see the old lag comedian doing his bit with the tatty old hats of empire. He harangues us with anxious grins and grimaces, eliciting a disconnected laughter from the disembodied studio audience. We are left to deal with a spatial and associative dislocation, only too aware of how pathetic has become the national culture the comedian hopelessly mimes.

A different hopelessness, a different dysfunction, informs Douglas Gordon's $10ms^{-1}$, 1994 (cat. 18). A large screen rests on the floor at a precarious angle to a vertical pole. On the screen flickers a projected image – uncertain, scratchy footage of a male figure, nearly naked, attempting, and failing, to stand up. The man's determined bearing and the suggestion of an iron bedstead in the background hint at a military context. This, and the apparent age of the film, make us think of the First World War, and the existentially fraught image turns political. Yet so much of Gordon's work to date has been concerned with the distortions to understanding created by uncertain memory. This must mean that my desire to read $10ms^{-1}$ as a piece about the sacrifice of ordinary working people during the last terrible gasp of a respectable British nationalism is simply overdetermined by the narrative flung up by the context of *The British Art Show 4*.

The selection process moved ahead. We met monthly and were slowly coming to an agreement about what was important for us. We had begun the process with a wide brief to fulfill. Such freedom of scope was disorienting in its own way as it meant our main guide had to be the distinctly individual and quite differing takes we each had on what was interesting. This meant we spent a fair amount of time discussing the overall shape of the exhibition we wanted. We looked at the pros and cons of older artists versus younger (in the end, a preference surfaced in favour of artists who emerged in the first five years of the 1990s), the desirability of commissioning work and the complexity of doing justice to a scene that relied to a great extent on the interpersonal dynamics of mixed shows organised by the participants. Although only a few British artists were touched by the frenzies of the 1980s art market, there were enough to infect all with a sense of excitement and possibility. But the economic benefits were so limited that people in Britain did not become dependent on ever-increasing sales as they did in hot gallery towns like New York and Cologne. Thus the collapse of the market in the early 1990s, which seems to have paralysed activity in New York, did not damage the collective psyche of British artists to such an extent. And, anyway, alternative strategies for showing work and circulating ideas have always been more a way of life here. Certainly in Britain these past five years or so there has been a clear trend of artists taking the initiative to organise shows – the legacy of Damien Hirst's *Freeze*, 1988, has reverberated throughout the period, as have the interventions of hit and run organisations like Rear Window. Along with this has been the growth of small, specialist spaces around London, places like Matt's Gallery, The Showroom, The Agency, and City Racing, which have concentrated on showing the newer work being done in London and around the country. These places in turn link up with more established collectives with strong local bases and a desire to reach a wider, international community, places like the revitalised Transmission in Glasgow.

In the end, practical considerations ruled our deliberations. We discussed how to acknowledge the force of these initiatives but the logistics of inviting a self-selected group of artists to interrupt our show with their own ultimately ruled against what might have been an exciting and risky alternative to the survey show. We also looked hard for a way to include performance art in the exhibition but, after considerable research and debate, resolved that it would be nearly impossible to accommodate. Again, the nature and variety of the gallery spaces available kept us thinking of site specific works, but a combination of factors began to move us away from that. Finally, we decided in favour of more movable installations, like those of Christine Borland, Mat Collishaw, Lucia Nogueira and Georgina Starr, installations that exist within an imaginary museum and are not dependent on the specifics of any one place to anchor meaning.

Midway through our discussions of the selection it became clear that the show we were designing relied to an unprecedented extent on new electronic technologies, especially new video projection capabilities. As this became apparent I came to feel under pressure to reconsider traditional categories of artmaking, with a special plea being made for the place of painting. This pressure gave me a lens with which to focus more clearly on the nature of our deliberations, and the quality of the decisions we had made to that point. This in turn confirmed the direction we had taken, and made me confident at least that we were on the right track.

The issue foregrounded by the painting question is that of post-modernity. What are the appropriate methods and responses for an artist today? Does it make sense to maintain rigid categories of work to address the transient world of the culture we inhabit, the culture of global consumerism? If we are all to some extent tourists to our own experience does it not make better sense to work episodically, glancing here and there as necessary rather than devotedly pursuing a singular craft? How to confront, or contest, the dominant desire for heterogeneous experiences? Can painting offer anything fresh at this historical moment? Or is it merely a throwback grimly loved by those who are mired in sentimentality for the modern. Can painting, alone, be deployed with irony, but not seem coy?

The best art being made in this country, regardless of medium, is actively informed and enlivened by a grasp of various cultural and political theories. But in the main the grasp is light and is leavened by a sense of humour. Yet perhaps because the idea of painting has become central to most arguments concerning the value and use of contemporary art, many painters, right now, seem encumbered and beleaguered.

How do the painters in the show relate to this? Hirst and Wallinger simply use the medium when it suits, treating painting almost as a prop, as a complex sign that mingles image and material and handling in a rich brew. This heady carnival of referencing, a vertigo of meaning, also occurs when an installation artist like Anya Gallaccio enriches her work with references to painting: the slow staining plane of red gerberas sandwiched between glass, the densely-brushed chocolate, the garishly-coloured flowers literally carpeting a woodland glade. Gallaccio's *Stroke*, 1994, a dark, pungent cell pregnant with conflicting significance, suggests both the euphoria of a chocolate binge and the claustrophobic terror of the 'dirty protest'. The Freudian-inspired identification of expressionist painting with an infantile fascination with human waste is now commonplace in art schools. Chris Ofili tackles this head on by placing giant elephant shits on the surface of his canvases, which he has prepared with dizzying patterns made up of tiny coloured spots. These patterns, so aggravating to the eye, seem inspired by the dream-time paintings of the aboriginal people of Australia, but the underlying images in Ofili's most recent work are based on William Blake's drawings for *Albion*. Thus a new kind of history painting is conceived, a hybrid that flushes rigorous categorical thinking down the plug hole of aesthetics.

By late May, the disorientation I was suffering as a result of jet lag had taken on the characteristics of a philosophy. The simple, straight-ahead task of getting from one place to another had so scrambled my senses that I moved as in a dream world. The pre-occupations of a day at work in studio or school would merge into the fitful consciousness of second-rate movies, forced meals and interrupted naps that constitutes jet travel, only to mix again with the stop and go of discussions in airless nooks and crannies dotted around the South Bank. It made perfect sense to me that the artists we were most interested in seemed fascinated by issues of emotional distress, psychic unease and identity confusion. It also suited my state of mind that they addressed these concerns with a deliberate heterogeneity of means that accepts newer technologies with an uncomplicated grace that challenges the relevance of the older categories of artmaking.

I think it is clear that the work in this exhibition is not content to sit quietly on the wall; it is attention-grabbing, eye-popping, ear-bending. Most of the works on display require an investment in time just to absorb what is on offer. Beyond that, the artists insist that we each think through the implications of what we see. But it is not always necessary for art to be large and complicated to make a complex point. As evidence here, witness the eloquent silence of Ceal Floyer's sneaky interventions in movie theatres around town, twiddling her thumbs as we look for greater meaning. The pleasures art offers are many, great and small. Sometimes they bring enlightenment, sometimes just a laugh or a squirm of delight. The point is that the pleasures are not there to be given, but for us to take.

Artists' biographies

COMPILED BY KATRINA CROOKALL

JORDAN BASEMAN

Born 1960, Philidelphia, USA

1979-83 BA Fine Art, Tyler School of Art, Temple University,
Pennsylvania
1986-88 MA Fine Art, Goldsmiths' College, London

Awards
1994 London Arts Board Award
1995 April/May. Artist in residence at Camden Arts Centre

One Person Exhibitions
1991 Alternative Arts, London
1993 Galerie Guy Ledune, Brussels
1994 Mario Flecha, London
Heber-Percy Gallery, Leamington Spa

Selected Group Exhibitions
1991 East Norwich Gallery
1992 East-South Norwich Gallery
Double Vision Vanessa Devereaux Gallery, London
Double Vision Anderson O'Day Gallery, London
Whitechapel Open Whitechapel Gallery, London
With Attitude (British Council) Galerie Guy Ledune
1993 The Peter Gabriel US Project London, Yokohama
1994 Vitrines Galerie Guy Ledune/Acte, Brussels
Curator's Egg Anthony Reynolds Gallery, London
Whitechapel Open Whitechapel Galley, London
1995 Composite Adj. Arnolfini, Bristol
Care and Control Rear Window at Hackney Hospital,
London
Fetishism National Touring Exhibitions from the
Hayward Gallery
Real Time Charlotte Road, London
Miniatures The Agency, London

CHRISTINE BORLAND

Born 1965, Darvel, Ayrshire

1983-87 BA Hons, Glasgow School of Art
1987-88 MA, University of Ulster, Belfast

One Person Exhibitions
1994 From Life Tramway, Glasgow
1995 From Life Kunst-Werke, Berlin
The British Council Gallery, Prague

Selected Group Exhibitions
1991 Kunst Europa Kunstverein Karlsruhe
Speed Transmission Gallery, Glasgow
The Living Room Project Curated by Giani Piacenti for his
Living Room, Glasgow
1992 Contact Transmission Gallery, Glasgow
Guilt by Association Irish Museum of Modern Art, Dublin
In and Out/Back and Forth 578 Broadway, New York
Artists Show Artists Galerie Vier, Berlin
1993 2 Person Exhibition Chisenhale Gallery, London
Underlay Spring St., Soho, New York
Aperto Venice Biennale
Fontanelle Kunstpeicher, Potsdam
2nd Tyne International Newcastle
Wonderful Life Lisson Gallery, London
Walter Benjamin's Briefcase Oporto
Left Luggage Rencontres dans un Couloir Hou Hanru,
Paris and tour
1994 The Spine De Appel Foundation, Amsterdam
Watt Witte de Witte Centre for Contemporary Art/
Kunsthal, Rotterdam
The Gaze Carré des Arts, Parc Florale de Paris
Ik & De Ander, Dignity for All: Reflections on Humanity Beurs
van Berlage, Amsterdam
East of Eden site specific works for castle and grounds,
Schloss Mosigkau, near Dessau
Riviera Group show of 5 Glasgow-based artists, Oriel
Mostyn, Llandudno
Little House On The Prairie Marc Jancou Gallery, London
Art Unlimited Arts Council Collection exhibition toured by
National Touring Exhibitions from the Hayward Gallery
Institute of Cultural Anxiety ICA, London
Heart of Darkness Kröller Müller Museum, Otterlo
1995 Eigen and Art at I.A.S. Independent Art Space, London
In Search of the Miraculous (In honour of Bas Jan Ader)
Starkmann Library Services, London
Wild Roses Grow By The Roadside 152 Brick Lane, London
S.W.A.R.M. The Scottish Arts Council Travelling Gallery
British Artists Museum Sztuki Lodz, Poland
Pulp Fact The Photographers' Gallery, London
50 Years Later The Shelter, Köln-Ehrenfeld, Cologne

MAT COLLISHAW

Born 1966, Nottingham

One Person Exhibitions
1990 Karsten Schubert, London
1992 Cohen Gallery, New York
1993 C.A.C. Maringy
      Galerie Analix, Geneva
      Raucci/Santamaria, Naples
1994 *The Eclipse of Venus* The Regency Palace Hotel, London

Selected Group Exhibitions
1991 *Stills and Switches* Zurich
1992 *Under 30* Galerie Metropol, Vienna
      Twenty Fragile Pieces Galerie Analix, Geneva
      Exhibit A Serpentine Gallery, London
      Collishaw, Fairhurst, Lane Via Farini, Milan
1993 *Aperto* Venice Biennale
      Changing 1 Dense Cities Shedalle, Zurich
1994 *L'Hiver de l'amour* Museum d'Art Modern, Ville de Paris
      Hellraiser Commune di Monte Carasso, Italy
      Not Self Portrait Karsten Schubert, London
1995 *Minky Manky* South London Gallery (curated by
        Carl Freedman)
      Corpus Delicti Kunstforeningen, Copenhagen

TACITA DEAN

Born 1965

1990-92 Slade School of Art, London

Awards
1992 BT New Contemporaries Award Winner
1993 Arts Council of Great Britain Film and Video Award
      Barclays Young Artist Award (runner-up)
1994 London Arts Board
1995 FRAC Award, Bourges, France

Selected Group Exhibitions
1992 *PG6* The Slade Gallery, London
      Six Slade Students Rijksademie, Amsterdam
1992-93 *BT New Contemporaries* Penzance, Manchester, Belfast, London
1993 *Barclays Young Artists* Serpentine Gallery, London
      Peripheral States Benjamin Rhodes Gallery, London
1994 *Watt* Witte de Witte Centre for Contemporary Art/
        Kunsthal, Rotterdam
      Coming Up For Air 144 Charing Cross Road/The Agency,
        London
      The Martyrdom of St Agatha and Other Stories Galerija Skuc,
        Ljubljana/Umetnostna Galerija, Maribor, Slovenia
      Mise-en-Scène ICA, London
1995 *Dew of Gold* Frith Street Gallery, London
      Hammoniale der Frauen Hamburg (with Tracy Emin, Jane
        and Louise Wilson, Gillian Wearing, Georgina Starr)

CEAL FLOYER

Born 1968, Karachi, Pakistan

1989-90 BA Theatre, Dartington College of Arts
1990-91 Art and Design Foundation Course, Sir John Cass
          School of Art and Design, London
1991-94 BA Fine Art, Goldsmiths' College, London

Selected Group Exhibitions
1992 *Hit & Run* Tufton St, London
1993 *Infanta of Castille* 194 Goldhawk Road, London
      Eye Witness Endeavour House, London
      Good Work Bonington Gallery, Nottingham
      Nosepaint Vauxhall Arches, London
      Fast Surface Chisenhale Gallery, London
1994 *Fast Forward* a site-specific projection commissioned by
        ICA Live Arts
      Making Mischief St James' St., London
      The City of Dreadful Night curated by Rear Window, Atlantis
        Lower Gallery, London
1995 The Showroom, London
      General Release Young British artists at Scuola di San
        Pasquale, Venice

JOHN FRANKLAND

Born 1961, Lancashire

1979 Rochdale College of Art
1980-83 BA Hons, Goldsmiths' College, London

Awards
1994 Thames Path Research Project

One Person Exhibitions
1993 *You can't touch this* Hales Gallery, London
1994 Hales Gallery, London

Selected Group Exhibitions
1991 *Ersatz 10* Martello Street, London
1992 *Whitechapel Open* Whitechapel Gallery, London
1994 *Tight* The Tannery, London Bridge
      Extension Bonington Gallery, Nottingham
1995 *Young British Artists IV* Saatchi Gallery, London

ANYA GALLACCIO

Born 1963, Glasgow

1985-88 BA, Goldsmiths' College, London

One Person Exhibitions
1991 Karsten Schubert, London
1992 *Small, Medium, Large* Karsten Schubert, London
        Red on Green ICA, London
1993 Kim Light Gallery, Los Angeles
        Ars Futura Galerie, Zurich
        Galerie Krinzinger, Vienna
        Home Alone (with Angus Fairhurst) 85 Charlotte St., London
1994 Stephania Miscetti, Rome
        Stroke Karsten Schubert, London
        Filiale Basel, Basel
        Stroke Blum and Poe Gallery, Los Angeles
1995 Bloom Gallery, Amsterdam
        Stephen Friedman Gallery, London
        Outdoor installation in Cowleaze Wood, outside Oxford
          (commissioned by Chiltern Sculpture Trail in 1993)

Selected Group Exhibitions
1991 *The Times, London's Young Artists* Art '91 Olympia, London
        Museum of Installation Site Three, Surrey Docks, London
        Broken English Serpentine Gallery, London
        Rachel Evans, Anya Gallaccio, Bridget Smith The Clove
          Building, London
1991-92 *Confrontaciones* Palacio Velasquez, Madrid
1992 *Fifth Anniversary Exhibition* Karsten Schubert, London
        15/1 Malania Basarab Gallery, London
        Life Size Museo d'Arte Contemporanea, Prato, Italy
        Barbara Gladstone Gallery and Stein Gladstone
          Gallery, New York (curated by Clarissa Dalrymple)
        *Sweet Home: Anya Gallaccio, Pat Kauffman, Cornelia Parker and
          Pat Thornton* Oriel Mostyn Gallery, Llandudno and tour
        20 Fragile Pieces Galerie Barbara et Luigi Polla, Geneva
        *With Attitude: Dominic Dennis, Anya Gallaccio and Simon
          Patterson* Galerie Rodolphe Janssen, Brussels
1993 *Ha-Ha* Spacex Gallery, Exeter
        Le Principe de Realité Villa Arson, Nice
        Mandy Loves Declan 100% Mark Boote Gallery, New York
        Le Jardin de la Vierge Musée Instrumental, Brussels
1994 *A Group Show* Karsten Schubert, London
        Punishment and Decoration Galerie Hohenthal and Bergen,
          Cologne (curated by Michael Corris)
        Domestic Violence Gio Marconi, Milan (curated by
          Alison Jacques)
        Choix de Bruxelles Espace Jacqmotte, Brussels
        Group Show: Gallery Artists Karsten Schubert, London
        inSITE94 Installation Gallery, San Diego and Tijuana, Mexico
        Sarah Staton Superstore Boutique . . . Laure Genillard Gallery,
          London
1995 *Art Unlimited* Arts Council Collection exhibition toured by
          National Touring Exhibitions from the Hayward Gallery
        Chocolate The Swiss Centre, New York
        Where you were even now Anya Gallaccio, Howard
          Hodgkin and Maggie Robert, Winterthor, Switzerland

DOUGLAS GORDON

Born 1966, Glasgow

1984-88 BA, Glasgow School of Art
1988-90 MA, Slade School of Art, London

One Person Exhibitions
1993 *24 Hour Psycho* Tramway, Glasgow and Kunst-Werke,
          Berlin
        Migrateur ARC, Musee d'Art Moderne de la Ville de Paris,
          Paris (curated by Hans Ulrich Obrist)
1994 Lisson Gallery, London
        Bad Faith Kunstlerhaus, Stuttgart
1995 *The End* Jack Tilton Gallery, New York
        24 Hour Psycho Kunstakedemie, Vienna

Selected Group Exhibitions
1991 *Barclays Young Artist Award* Serpentine Gallery, London
        The Bellgrove Station Billboard Project Glasgow
        Windfall '91 Seamen's Mission, Glasgow
        Walk On Jack Tilton Gallery, New York and Fruitmarket
          Gallery, Edinburgh
1992 *A Modest Proposal* Milch Gallery, London
        Love At First Sight The Showroom, London
        Guilt by Association Museum of Modern Art, Dublin
        And What Do You Represent? Anthony Reynolds Gallery,
          London
        Speaker Project ICA, London
        Anomie Patent House/Andrew Cross, London
        L, u di carte Cafe Picasso, Rome
        Five Dialogues The Museum of Natural History, Bergen
        240 Minuten Galerie Esther Schipper, Cologne
        Il Mistero dei 100 Dollari Scomparsi Gio' Marconi, Milan
1993 *Left Luggage* Rencontres dans un Couloir Hou Hanru,
          Paris and tour
        Prospekt 93 Kunsthalle, Frankfurt
        Douglas Gordon and Simon Patterson Gallery Gruppe Grun,
          Bremen
        Wonderful Life Lisson Gallery, London
        Viennese Story Wiener Secession, Vienna
        Walter Benjamin's Briefcase Moagens Harmonia, Oporto
          (curated by Andrew Renton)
        Chambre 763 Hotel Carlton Palace, Paris
        High Fidelity Kohji Ogura Gallery, Nagoya and Rontgen
          Gallery, Tokyo
        Before the sound of the beep soundworks, throughout Paris
        Purpose Built . . . Real Art Ways, Hartford, Connecticut
        Instructions Studio Marconi, Milan
1994 *Stains in Reality* Gallerie Nicolai Wallner, Copenhagen
        Wall to Wall National Touring Exhibition from the
          Hayward Gallery
        The Reading Room Oxford (initiated by Bookworks, London)
        Modern Art Transmission Gallery, Glasgow
        Conceptual Living Rhizome, Amsterdam
        Institute of Cultural Anxiety ICA, London (curated by
          Jeremy Millar)
        Watt at Witte de Witte Centre for Contemporary Art/
          Kunsthal, Rotterdam

New European Video Screenings Centre Georges Pompidou,
  Paris
Points de Vue: Images d'Europe Centre Georges Pompidou,
  Paris
1995 *Young British Artists Eigen + Art* at IAS, London
Kopfbanhof Liepzig Banhof (curated by Gerti Fietzek)
Every Time I See You Gallerie Nicolai Wallner, Malmö
Take Me (I'm Yours) Serpentine Gallery, London (curated by
  Hans Ulrich Obrist)
General Release Young British artists at Scuola di San
  Pasquale, Venice

DAMIEN HIRST

Born 1965, Bristol

1983-85 Jacob Kramer College of Art, Leeds
1986-89 BA, Goldsmiths' College, London

Awards
1995 Prix Eliette von Karajan '95, Salzburg

One Person Exhibitions
1991 *In & Out of Love* Woodstock St, London
When Logic Dies Emmanuel Perrotin, Paris
Internal Affairs ICA, London
1992 *Where's God Now* Jay and Donatella Chiat, New York
Marianne, Hildegarde Unfair, Jay Jopling, Cologne
Pharmacy Cohen Gallery, New York
1993 *Visual Candy* Regen Projects Los Angeles
Damien Hirst Galerie Jablonka, Cologne
1994 *Making Beautiful Drawings* Bruno Brunnet, Berlin
Current 23 Milwaukee Art Museum
A Bad Environment for White Monochrome Paintings Mattress
  Factory, Pittsburgh
A Good Environment for Coloured Monochrome Paintings DAAD
  Gallery, Berlin
Pharmacy Dallas Museum, Dallas
1995 *Pharmacy* Kukje Gallery, Seoul
Still Whitecube/Jay Jopling, London
Damien Hirst Gagosian Gallery, New York

Selected Group Exhibitions
1991 *Louder Than Words* The Cornerhouse, Manchester
Broken English Serpentine Gallery, London
1992 *Young British Artists* Saatchi Collection, London
Made for Arolsen Arolsen, Germany
Moltiplici/Cultura Rome
London Portfolio Karsten Schubert, London
Post Human Fondation Asher Edelman, Lausanne
Group Show Lois Campana Gallery, Frankfurt
Strange Developments Anthony d'Offay Gallery, London
British Art Barbara Gladstone Gallery, New York
Avantgarde & Kampagne Stadtische Kunsthalle, Dusseldorf
Turkish Biennial Istanbul
Turner Prize Exhibition Tate Gallery, London
Under Thirty Galerie Metropol, Vienna

1993 *The 21st Century* Kunsthalle, Basle
The Nightshade Family Museum Friedericianum, Kassel
Aperto Venice Biennale
Displace Cohen Gallery, New York
A Wonderful Life Lisson Gallery, London
1994 *Some Went Mad, Some Ran Away* Serpentine Gallery, London
  and tour
Domestic Violence Gio Marconi, Milan
Virtual Reality National Gallery of Australia, Canberra
Cocido y Crudo Reina Sofia, Madrid
Nature Morte Tanya Bonakdar Gallery, New York
Art Unlimited Arts Council Collection exhibition toured by
  National Touring Exhibitions from the Hayward Gallery
From Beyond the Pale Irish Museum of Modern Art, Dublin
1995 *Drawing the Line* National Touring Exhibitions from the
  Hayward Gallery
Signs and Wonders Kunsthaus, Zurich
Minky Manky South London Gallery (curated by Carl
  Freedman)
From Here Waddington Galleries/Karsten Schubert, London
Group Show Bruno Brunnet Galerie, Berlin

GARY HUME

Born 1962, Kent

1985-88 Goldsmiths' College of Art, London

One Person Exhibitions

1991 *Recent Works* Karsten Schubert, London
The Dolphin Paintings Karsten Schubert, London
Tarpaulins Galerie Tanja Grunert, Cologne
1992 *Recent Paintings* Matthew Marks, New York
Recent Paintings Daniel Weinberg Gallery, Santa Monica
1993 Galerie Tanja Grunert, Cologne
1994 Matthew Marks, New York
1995 ICA, London
Kunsthalle, Berne
Jay Jopling/White Cube, London

Selected Group Exhibitions

1991 *Group Show* Karsten Schubert, London
Artists Sketchbooks Matthew Marks, New York
Summer Show Matthew Marks, New York
Broken English Serpentine Gallery, London
Act-up Benefit Paula Cooper Gallery, New York
1991-92 *Confrontaciones* Palacio Valasquez, Madrid
1992 *5th Anniversary Show* Karsten Schubert, London
Etats Specifique Musée des Beaux-Arts, Le Havre
Summer Show Karsten Schubert, London
Summer Show Matthew Marks, New York
New Voices: New Works British Council Collection,
Centre de Conference, Brussels
Group Show Barbara Gladstone Gallery, New York (curated
by Clarissa Dalrymple)
Group Show Galerie Tanja Grunert, Cologne
Il Mistero dei 100 Dollari Scomparsi Gio Marconi Gallery,
Milan
1993 *New Voices* Musée National d'Histoire, Luxemburg
Lucky Kunst New York/London
Wonderful Life Lisson Gallery, London
Spit in the Ocean Anthony Reynolds Gallery, London
Close Up Time Square, New York
1994 *Not Self-Portrait* Karsten Schubert, London
Beauty is Fluid P.P.Q., London
Unbound Hayward Gallery, London
1995 *Brilliant! New Art From London* Walker Arts Center,
Minneapolis
From Here Waddington Galleries/Karsten Schubert, London
Minky Manky South London Gallery (curated by
Carl Freedman)
General Release Young British artists at Scuola di San
Pasquale, Venice

PERMINDAR KAUR

Born 1965, Nottingham

1986-89 BA in Fine Art, Sheffield City Polytechnic
1990-92 MA in Fine Art, Glasgow School of Art

Awards

1994 First Prize, Salo D'Arts Plastiques Baix Camp, Reus
Visual Arts Grant, The British Council
1995 Banff Centre for the Arts, Calgary

One Person Exhibitions

1993 *Red Earth* Harris Museum & Art Gallery, Preston
Regions & Growth The British Council, Barcelona
1994 Galleri Amidol, Gothenburg, Sweden (collaborative work
with Peter Lundh)
Hidden Witnesses Galleri Amidol, Gothenburg
1995 *Små Utrymmen* Galleri Isidor, Malmö, Sweden

Selected Group Exhibitions

1991 *Salon Der Debutanten* Slagharen, Holland
*Starting Points: Towards An International Exhibition Concerning
Issues of Local Identity* Mappin Art Gallery, Sheffield
Artful Europe Niort, France
Interim Newberry Gallery, Glasgow
Four x 4 Arnolfini, Bristol
1992 *Narratives* Mappin Art Gallery, Sheffield
Invisible Cities Fruitmarket Gallery, Edinburgh
BBC Billboard Art Project Glasgow
BT New Contemporaries Newlyn Orion Gallery, Penzance
and tour
MA Fine Art Show Centre for Developmental Arts, Glasgow
Taking Flight Leicester City Art Gallery and tour
1993 *Asian Arts Festival* Worcester City Art Gallery
Group Show El Diento Del Tiempo, Valencia
Artifici Galerie Maria Jose Castevellvi, Barcelona
1994 *La Cambra Daurada* La Capella de l'Antic Hospital de la
Santa Creu, Barcelona
Panfletos de Agri-cultura poster project organised by
Transformadors, Barcelona
Escletxes Espais, Girona (with Pep Aymerich and Toni Giro)
Project for Europe Ferry Kronberg, Copenhagen and British
Council tour
La Cambra Daurada Arteleku, San Sebastian
1995 *My Bloody Valentine* Real AA Foundation, Barcelona
por al buit/miedo al vacio Galeria Carles Poy, Barcelona
Veins Galeria dels Angels, Barcelona

STEVE McQUEEN

Born 1969, London

1989-90   Chelsea School of Art, London
1990-93   Goldsmiths' College, London
1993-94   Tisch School of the Arts, New York University

Selected Group Exhibitions
1994   *Acting Out: The Body in Video* Then and Now Royal College
           of Art, London
1995   *Mirage: Enigma of Race, Difference and Desire* ICA, London

LUCIA NOGUEIRA

Born 1950, Goiania, Brazil

1976-79   Chelsea School of Art, London
1979-80   Central School of Art, London
   1993   Residency, Fondation Cartier, Paris

One Person Exhibitions
1992   Anthony Reynolds Gallery, London
           The left hand does not know what the right hand does Espace
              Artere Sud, Brussels
1993   Ikon Gallery, Birmingham
1994   Camden Arts Centre, London
1995   Anthony Reynolds Gallery, London

Selected Group Exhibitions
1991   *Gulliver's Travels* Galerie Sophie Ungers, Cologne
           Gymnopedies Galerie Angels de la Motta, Barcelona
1993   *WaterCOLOUR* Curwen Gallery, London
           Spit in the Ocean Anthony Reynolds Gallery, London
           Singer Friedlander Watercolour Exhibition Mall Galleries,
              London
1994   Anthony Reynolds Gallery, London
           Le Shuttle Kunstlerhaus Bethanien, Berlin
           Untitled Streamer Eddy Monkley Full Stop Etcetera Anthony
              Reynolds Gallery, London
1995   *Here and Now* Serpentine Gallery, London

CHRIS OFILI

Born 1968, Manchester

1987-88   Thameside College of Technology, Ashton-under-Lyne
1988-91   BA (Hons) Fine Art, Chelsea School of Art, London
1991-93   MA in Painting, Royal College of Art, London

Awards
1992   Erasmus Exchange to Berlin, Germany
           British Council Travel Scholarship, Zimbabwe
1993   Second Prizewinner, Tokyo Print Biennale

One Person Exhibitions
1991   *Paintings and Drawings* Kepler Gallery, London

Selected Group Exhibitions
1991   *Whitworth Young Contemporaries* (prizewinner) Whitworth
              Art Gallery, Manchester
           BP Portrait Award National Portrait Gallery, London
           Blauer Montag Raum fur Kunst, Basle (curated by
              Killian Dellers)
           Top Marks London Institute Galleries, London
1992-93   *Pachipamwe International* Bulawayo Art Gallery, Zimbabwe;
              National Gallery, Harare
1993   *Art Fair '93* Business Design Centre, London
           Borderless Print Rochdale Art Gallery (curated by
              Maud Sulter)
           To Boldly Go . . . Cubitt St. Gallery, London (curated by
              Stuart Morgan)
           Shit Sale Strasse 17 Juni, Berlin
           Shit Sale Brick Lane, London
           Group Show Paton Gallery, London
           Riverside Open Riverside Gallery, London
           Tokyo Print Biennale Machida-City Museum, Tokyo
           New Art Award Cubitt St. Gallery, London
           Lift Atlantis Basement, London
           BT New Contemporaries Cornerhouse Gallery, Manchester
              and tour
1994   *Miniatures* The Agency, London
           Take Five Anthony Wilkinson Fine Art, London
           Painting Show Victoria Miro Gallery, London
1995   *A Bonnie Situation* Contemporary Fine Arts, Berlin
           Selections Spring '95 The Drawing Centre, New York
           Contained Cultural Instructions, London
           Im/Pure Osterwalder's Art Office, Hamburg (curated by
              Glenn Scott-Wright)

JULIE ROBERTS

Born 1963, Fflint, Wales

1980-84 HND, Wrexham School of Art, Wales
1986-87 St. Martin's School of Art, London
1988-90 MA Fine Art, Glasgow School of Art

Awards
1992 British Council Scholarship, Budapest

One Person Exhibitions
1992 James Hockey Gallery, Farnham
Centre for Contemporary Art, Glasgow
1993 Interim Art, London
1995 Gallerie Ghislaine Hussenot, Paris
Wall Paintings Interim Art, London

Selected Group Exhibitions
1991 *Bellgrove Station Billboard Project* Glasgow
Speed Transmission Gallery, Glasgow
Windfall '91 Glasgow
1992 *Critic's Choice* The Cooling's Gallery, London
Love At First Sight The Showroom, London
Transmission at City Racing City Racing, London
Unfair Cologne
1993 *Aperto* Venice Biennale
Painting Invitational Barbara Gladstone Gallery, New York
Left Luggage Rencontres dans un Couloir Hou Hanru, Paris and tour
1994 *Art Oriente Objet* MA Galerie, Paris
Julie Roberts, Trudie Reiss, Elke Krystufek Galerie Meile, Lucerne
Wall to Wall National Touring Exhibition from the Hayward Gallery
Choix de Bruxelles Galerie Rodolphe Janssen, Brussels
Five British Artists Andréhn-Schiptjenko, Stockholm (with Jake and Dinos Chapman, Simon Patterson and Mark Wallinger)
Redefining the Art Icon Pamela Auchincloss Gallery, New York
Modern Art Transmission Gallery, Glasgow
Riviera Seven Artists from Scotland, Oriel Mostyn, Llandudno
Don't Wake Up Interim Art, London
Conceptual Living Amsterdam (Rhizome)
Galerie Meile (with Elke Krystufek and Trudie Reiss)
Julie Roberts, Damien Hirst, Mat Collishaw, Stephen Murphy Tanya Bonakdar Gallery, New York
1995-96 *S.W.A.R.M.* Scottish Arts Council Travelling Gallery

BRIDGET SMITH

Born 1966, Southend on Sea

1984-85 Central School of Art, London
1985-88 Goldsmiths' College, London

Awards
1991 GLA Women's Photography Award

One Person Exhibitions
1995 Entwistle Contemporary, London

Selected Group Exhibitions
1991 *Rachel Evans, Anya Gallaccio, Bridget Smith* Clove Gallery, London
1992 *Hit & Run* Tufton St, London
Love at First Sight The Showroom, London
1993 *Wonderful Life* Lisson Gallery, London
Time Out Billboard Project London
Tony Hayward, Jaki Irvine, Ian Pratt, Bridget Smith Riverside, London
1994 *!GOL!* Mark Boote Gallery, New York
The Event 152c Brick Lane, London
Close Encounters Ikon Gallery, Birmingham
Institute of Cultural Anxiety: Works from the Collection ICA, London
1995 *Having It* Spital Studio, London
Something Cheap Custard Factory, Birmingham
Räumefür Neve Kunft Rolf Henges Bach, Wuppertal

GEORGINA STARR

Born 1968, Leeds

1987-90 Middlesex Polytechnic
1990-92 Slade School of Art, London
1993-94 Rijksakademie Van Beeldende Kunst, Amsterdam

Awards
1991 British Institute Award for Sculpture
Duveen travel Award
1993 VSB Bank Award
Leverhulme Trust Award
Uriot Prize

One Person Exhibitions
1992 *Mentioning* Anthony Reynolds Gallery, London
1994 *Getting to Know You* Anthony Reynolds Gallery, London
(Un)Controlling Stedlijk Museum Bureau, Amsterdam
Seventh Museum Stroom, Den Haag
Crying Galerie Krinzinger, Vienna
1995 *Visit to a Small Planet* Kunsthalle, Zurich
Bloom Gallery, Amsterdam
Art Now Tate Gallery, London

Selected Group Exhibitions

1991 *A.V.E. 91 Filmuis*, Arnhem

1992 *P.G.6.* Slade Gallery, London
Through View Diorama Gallery, London

1993 *Barclays Young Artists* Serpentine Gallery, London
Aperto Venice Biennale
Ha-Ha Spacex, Exeter
Wonderful Life Lisson Gallery, London
Restaurant La Bocca, Paris
High Fidelity Kohji Ogura Gallery, Nagoya
Open Atellerdagen Rijksakademie, Amsterdam

1994 *High Fidelity* The Rontgen Kunst Institut, Tokyo
Andrea Rosen Gallery, New York
Looking at Words: Reading Pictures Elms Lester, London
and tour
Without Walls The Face Magazine
WM Karaoke Portikus, Frankfurt
Europa 94 Munich
Untitled Streamer Eddy Monkley Full Stop Etcetera Anthony
Reynolds Gallery, London
Le Shuttle Kunstlerhaus Bethanien, Berlin
Schipper & Krome, Cologne
Electric Ladyland Jusse Seguin, Paris
Points de vue (Images d'Europe) Centre Georges Pompidou,
Paris
Use Your Allusion; Recent Video Art Museum of Contemporary
Art, Chicago
It's how you play the game Exit Art, New York

1995 Kunstforeningen, Copenhagen
Anthony Reynolds Gallery, London
Hopeless Centre for Contemporary Art, Glasgow
In Search of the Miraculous Starkmann Ltd., London
Every Time I See You Nicolai Wallner, Malmö
La Valise du Celibataire Maastricht
Couldn't get ahead I.A.S., London
Campo Venice Biennale
Here and Now Serpentine Gallery
Wild Walls Stedelijk Museum, Amsterdam
Brilliant! New Art From London Walker Art Center,
Minneapolis

KERRY STEWART

Born 1965, Paisley, Scotland

1985-89 MA German and History of Art, Edinburgh University
1989-90 Chelsea School of Art, London
1990-93 BA Sculpture, Chelsea School of Art, London

Awards

1993 Swiss Government Postgraduate Scholarship, Basle

One Person Exhibitions

1995 Yorkshire Sculpture Park, Wakefield, Yorkshire

Selected Group Exhibitions

1992 *Sweet Rice* Elephant and Castle, London
Flou Les Ets Phonographiques, Paris

1993 *Riverside Open* Riverside Studios, London
Whitworth Young Contemporaries Whitworth Art Gallery,
Manchester
BT New Contemporaries Cornerhouse, Manchester and tour

1994 *No Vacancies* Frankfurt, Germany

1995 *City Racing*, London (with Peter Owen)
In and Out of Touch Budapest, Hungary
In and Out of Touch Hans Ungarn, Berlin
Young British Artists IV Saatchi Gallery, London

MARCUS TAYLOR

Born 1964, Belfast

1982 Ulster Polytechnic, Belfast
1986 Camberwell School of Art, London
1988 Slade School of Art, London

Awards

1995-96 Berwick upon Tweed Gymnasiun Fellowship

One Person Exhibitions

1992 Jay Jopling, London

1993 Jean Bernier, Athens
Xavier Hufkens, Brussels
White Cube, London
Bruno Brunnet, Berlin

1994 Galerie Samia Saouma, Paris
Kerlin Gallery, Dublin

Selected Group Exhibitions

1992 *London Portfolio* Karsten Schubert, London
British Art Barbara Gladstone Gallery, New York

1995 *Young British Artists IV* Saatchi Gallery, London
Life Patterns Tate Gallery, London

SAM TAYLOR-WOOD

Born 1967, London

1987-88   North East London Polytechnic
1988-90   BA (Hons) Fine Art, Goldsmiths' College, London

One Person Exhibitions
1994   The Showroom, London
1995   Galleri Andreas Brandström, Stockholm

Selected Group Exhibitions
1991   *Show Hide Show* Anderson O'Day Gallery, London
          (curated by Andrew Renton)
1992   Clove Two Gallery, London
1993   *Information* Deinst Kunsthalle, Stuttgart
          (touring exhibition)
          Wonderful Life Lisson Gallery, London
          Lucky Kunst Silver Place, Soho, London
          Close Up Times Square, New York
          Annihilation Victoria Miro Gallery, London
          Knock 'em Dead PPQ, HQ, London
1994   *Don't Look Now* Thread Waxing Space, New York
          (curated by Joshua Dector)
          Not Self-Portrait Karsten Schubert, London
          Curator's Egg Anthony Reynolds Gallery, London
          Other Men's Flowers Paragon Press/Factual Nonsense,
          London
1995   *Corpus Delicti* Kunstforeningen, Copenhagen
          Group Show Galerie Michel Rein, Tours
          Young British Artists Project for General Release, Venice
          Biennale
          Aperto '95 Le Nouveau Musée, Villeurbanne, France
          Stoppage CCC Tours, Tours
          Brilliant! New Art From London Walker Art Center,
          Minneapolis
          Perfect Speed Toronto and tour (curated by Catsou Roberts)

MARK WALLINGER

Born 1959, Chigwell, Essex

1978-81   Chelsea School of Art, London
1983-85   MA, Goldsmiths' College, London

One Person Exhibitions
1991   *Capital* Grey Art Gallery, New York; Daniel Newburg
          Gallery, New York
          Capital ICA, London and tour
1992   *Fountain* Anthony Reynolds Gallery, London
1993   Daniel Newburg Gallery, New York
1994   *The Full English* Anthony Reynolds Gallery, London
1995   *A Real Work of Art* Galerie Buchmann, Basle; Ikon Gallery,
          Birmingham

Selected Group Exhibitions
1991   *Kunstlandshaft Europa* Kunstverein Karlsruhe
          Confrontaciones Palacio de Velasquez, Madrid
1992   *Whitechapel Open* Clove Building, London
          Let Me Look San Miniato
1993   *Young British Artists II* Saatchi Collection, London
          Spit in the Ocean Anthony Reynolds Gallery, London
          You've Tried the Rest, Now Try the Best City Racing, London
          Mandy Loves Declan 100% Mark Boote Gallery, New York
          MA Galerie, Paris
          Young British Artists from the Saatchi Collection Cologne
1994   *Jet Lag* Galerie Martina Detterer, Frankfurt
          Every Now And Then Rear Window/Richard Salmon,
          London
          Not Self Portrait Karsten Schubert Gallery, London
          Five British Artists Galleri Andréhn-Schiptjenko, Stockholm
          Here and Now Serpentine Gallery, London
          Untitled Steamer Eddy Monkey Full Stop Etcetera Anthony
          Reynolds Gallery, London
          Sarah Stanton's Supastore Boutique Laure Genillard Gallery,
          London
          Seeing the Unseen 30 Shepherdess Walk, London
          Idea Europa Palazzo Publico, Siena
          A Painting Show Deweer Art Gallery, Otegem
          Art Unlimited Arts Council Collection exhibition toured by
          National Touring Exhibitions from the Hayward Gallery
1995   *The Art Casino* Barbican Art Gallery, London

GILLIAN WEARING

Born 1963, Birmingham

1985-87 B TECH Art and Design, Chelsea School of Art, London
1987-90 BA (Hons) Fine Art, Goldsmiths' College, London

Awards
1993-94 BT Young Contemporaries

One Person Exhibitions
1993 City Racing, London
1994 Interim Art, London
1995 Basilico Fine Arts, New York
      Western Security Hayward Gallery, London

Selected Group Exhibitions
1991 *Empty Gestures* Diorama Art Centre, London
      Clove I The Clove Building, London
      Piece Talks Diorama Art Centre, London
1992 *British Art Group Show* Le Musée des Beaux Arts dans
         le Havre, France
      Instruction Marconi Gallery, Milan
1993 *Vox Pop* Laure Genillard Gallery, London
      2 into 1 Centre 181 Gallery, London
      Mandy Loves Declan 100% Mark Boote Gallery, New York
      Okay Behaviour 303 Gallery, New York
      BT Young Contemporaries Cornerhouse, Manchester and tour
1994 *Not Self Portrait* Karsten Schubert Gallery, London
      R.A.S. Galerie Analix, Geneva (curated by Gianni Romano)
      Domestic Violence Gio Marconi, Milan (curated by
         Alison Jacques)
      Fuori Fase Via Farini, Milan
      Uncertain Identity Galerie Analix, Geneva
      3.016.026 Theoretical Events, Naples
      Le Shuttle Kunstlerhaus Bethanien, Berlin
1995 *Campo* Venice Biennale (curated by Francesco Bonami)
      Sage Michel Rien, Tours
      It's not a picture Galleria Emi Fontana, Milan
      Brilliant! New Art from London Walker Art Center,
         Minneapolis
      Mysterium Alltag Kampnagel, Hamburg (with Jane and
         Louise Wilson, Tacita Dean, Tracey Emin)
      Aperto '95 Nouveau Musée, Institut d'Art Contemporain,
         Villeurbanne, France
      Hotel Mama (Aperto '95) Kunstraum, Vienna
      Make Believe Royal College of Art, London
      Mobius Strip Basilico Fine Arts, New York
      Hello! Andréhn-Schiptjenko, Stockholm
      Gone Blum & Poe, Los Angeles (with Bas Jan Ader, Sam
         Durant, Rainer Ganahl)

JANE AND LOUISE WILSON

JANE WILSON

Born 1967

1986-89 BA Fine Art, Newcastle Polytechnic
1990-92 MA Fine Art, Goldsmiths' College, London

Awards
1993 Barclays Young Artist Award

LOUISE WILSON

Born 1967

1986-89 BA Fine Art, Duncan of Jordanstone College of Art,
         Dundee
1990-92 MA Fine Art, Goldsmiths' College, London

Awards
1993 Barclays Young Artist Award

Two Person Exhibitions
1994 *Routes 1 & 9 North* AC Project Room, New York
      Crawl Space British Project II, Galerie Krinzinger, Vienna

Selected Group Exhibitions
1992 *Summer Show* Laure Genillard Gallery, London
      Into the Nineties 4 Mall Galleries, London
1993 *Barclays Young Artists* Serpentine Gallery, London
      Underlay Renwick St., New York
      The Daily Planet Transmission Gallery, Glasgow
      Over the Limit Arnolfini, Bristol
      BT Young Contemporaries Cornerhouse, Manchester and tour
      Summer Show David Zwirner Gallery, New York
      Wonderful Life Lisson Gallery, London
      Lucky Kunst Silver Place, Soho, London
      Close Up 42nd Street, New York
      Walter Benjamin's Briefcase Moagens, Oporto (curated by
         Andrew Renton)
      Beyond Belief Lisson Gallery, London
1994 *Domestic Violence* Gio Marconi, Milan; Galerie 102,
         Dusseldorf
      New Reality Mix 18 Högbergsgatan, Stockholm
      The Ecstacy of Limits Gallery 400, University of Illinois,
         Chicago
      Le Shuttle Kunstlerhaus Bethanian, Berlin
      Facts of Life Gallerie 102, Dusseldorf and tour
      Use Your Allusion: Recent Video Art MCA, Chicago
1995 *Young British Artists* Eigen + Art at IAS, London
      Corpus Delicti Kunstforeningen, Copenhagen
      General Release Young British artists at Scuola di San
         Pasquale, Venice

HERMIONE WILTSHIRE

Born 1963, London

1982-85 Central School of Art, London
1986-87 Chelsea School of Art, London

Awards
1991 G.L.A. Production Awards
1994 L.A.B. Production Award

One/Two Person Exhibitions
1991 Riverside Studios, London
1992 Lisson Gallery, London
1994 O2 (with Helen Chadwick) Zone Gallery, Newcastle
       Lost at Sea and Found on the Ground Eugen Lendl Gallerie, Graz
       A Pressing Engagement British Council Window Gallery, Prague

Selected Group Exhibitions
1992 *Addressing the Forbidden* Brighton Festival (toured to Stills Gallery, Edinburgh)
       Traces of the Figure City Museum and Gallery, Stoke-on-Trent and tour
1993 *Sweet Side Show* (in collaboration with Emilyn Claid, dancer) Riverside Studios, London
       Elective Affinities Tate Gallery, Liverpool
       Itself Transmission Gallery, Glasgow
       What She Wants toured throughout Britain
1994 *Thinking Aloud* Small Mansion Arts Centre, London
       It's a Pleasure Royal Festival Hall, London
1995 *U.K. Wit and Excess* Contemporary Art Centre of South Australia, Adelaide (toured throughout Australia)
       British Art of the 80's and 90's The Weltkunst Collection, Irish Museum of Modern Art, Dublin
       Summer Exhibition Gimpel Fils, London

CATHERINE YASS

Born 1963, London

1982-86 BA, Slade School of Art, London
1984-85 Hochschule der Kunst, Berlin
1989-90 MA, Goldsmiths' College, London

One Person Exhibitions
1991 Tavistock Centre for Psychotherapy, London
1992 Laure Genillard Gallery, London
1994 Viewpoint Gallery, Salford, Manchester
       Heber-Percy Gallery, Leamington Spa

Selected Group Exhibitions
1991 Clove Building, Butler's Wharf, London
       The Times, London's Young Artists Art '91, Olympia, London
       Sign of the Times Camerawork, London
1992 *Anomie* Patent House, London
       Discretion Canary Wharf, London
       Brit Art Kunsthaus, Glarus
       Exhibit A Serpentine Gallery, London
1993 *Inner Side* Architectural Association, London
       Vox Pop Laure Genillard Gallery, London
1994 Galerie Martina Detterer, Frankfurt
       Whitechapel Open Whitechapel Art Gallery, London

List of Works

JORDAN BASEMAN

1 **Manifest Destiny** 1995
Baby's bib and human hair
25 x 50 cm
Courtesy of Saatchi Collection,
London

2 **Moist Secret** 1995
Wax cast of human tongue and
oil paint
6 x 6 x 3 cm
Courtesy of Saatchi Collection,
London

3 **Shoes (Size 8)** 1995
Leather and cork
84 x 74 x 13 cm
Courtesy of Saatchi Collection,
London

4 **Words Will Never Hurt Me** 1995
Children's shirts, human hair
152 x 91 x 457 cm
Commissioned by Camden Arts
Centre, courtesy of the artist

CHRISTINE BORLAND

5 **Black Museum** 1994
Portakabin and objects: men's
suit jacket, house plants, bullet-
proof lining, neck tie, prisoners'
heads, distressed surfaces,
defence injury, stairwell-running,
falling, rising, the ground
673 x 287 cm
Courtesy of the artist

MAT COLLISHAW

6 **Antique** 1994
Video projection, glass and wood
33 x 183 cm
Courtesy of Art & Public, Geneva

7 **Snowstorm** 1994
Video installation
35.6 x 28 cm
Courtesy of Galerie Analix -
B & L Polla, Geneva

8 **Song Cycle** 1994
8 budgerigars, 2 reel to reel tape
recorders, 2 microphones, 2
speaker cabinets, cage
200 x 200 x 400 cm
Courtesy of Galerie Analix - B & L
Polla, Geneva

9 **Untitled** 1994
Plastic, lights and fittings, C-type
photographs
20 x 30.5 cm
Courtesy of Galerie Analix -
B & L Polla, Geneva

TACITA DEAN

10 **Martyrdom of St Agatha
(in several parts)** 1994
16mm film
13 mins, 5 secs
Courtesy of Frith Street Gallery

11 **Girl Stowaway** 1995
Installation
Dimensions variable
Courtesy of Frith Street Gallery

CEAL FLOYER

12 **Light Switch** 1992
Slide projection
10 x 10 cm
Courtesy of the artist

13 **Light** 1994
Disconnected light bulb and flex,
4 slide projectors
Dimensions variable
Courtesy of the artist

14 **Minute** 1995
Cinema intervention
35 mm film (1 min)
Courtesy of the artist

JOHN FRANKLAND

15 **Untitled (Shed)** 1994
Laminated polythene, wood
245 x 244 x 184 cm
Courtesy of Saatchi Collection,
London

ANYA GALLACCIO

16 **Installation** 1995
Chocolate
Dimensions variable
Courtesy of the artist

17 **Preserve (Beauty)** 1995
Gerberas and glass
Dimensions variable
Courtesy of the artist

DOUGLAS GORDON

18 **10ms^{-1}** 1994
Video installation
228.5 x 306 cm
Courtesy of The British Council

19 **Hysterical** 1995
Video installation
400 x 300 cm (x 2)
Courtesy of Contemporary Art
Society

DAMIEN HIRST

20 **He Tried to Internalise
Everything** 1992-94
Glass, steel, table, chair and gas
compressor
213 x 213 x 305 cm
Courtesy of Jay Jopling, London

21 **Away from the Flock** 1994
Steel, glass, formaldehyde
solution and lamb
96 x 149 x 51 cm
Courtesy of Saatchi Collection,
London

22 **I Feel Love** 1994/95
Gloss household paint and
butterflies on canvas
274 x 274 cm
Courtesy of Jay Jopling, London

23 **I Love, Love** 1994/95
Gloss household paint and
butterflies on canvas
274 x 274 cm
Courtesy of Jay Jopling, London

GARY HUME

24 **After Petrus Christus** 1994
Gloss household paint on board
122 x 76 cm
Courtesy of Jay Jopling, London

25 **Baby** 1995
Enamel paint on aluminium
173 x 173 cm
Courtesy of Jay Jopling, London

26 **Flying** 1995
Enamel paint on aluminium
198 x 150 cm
Courtesy of the artist

27 **Four Feet in the Garden** 1995
Enamel paint on aluminium
221 x 170 cm
Courtesy of Arts Council
Collection

28 **Funny Girl** 1995
Enamel paint on aluminium
198 x 150 cm
Courtesy of Private Collection,
London

PERMINDAR KAUR

29 **Innocence** 1993
Cloth and iron
60 x 70 cm
Courtesy of the artist

30 **Untitled** 1993
Cloth and iron
50 x 177 x 62 cm
Courtesy of the artist

31 **Cot** 1994
Fabric and steel
150 x 105 x 62 cm
Courtesy of Museu Comarcal
Salvador Vilaseca, Reus

32 **Untitled** 1994
Fabric
30 x 120 x 80 cm
Courtesy of the artist

33 **Untitled** 1995
Fabric and copper
120 x 60 x 20 cm
Courtesy of Private Collection,
Sweden

STEVE McQUEEN

34 **Bear** 1993
16mm film, video transfer
The artist, courtesy of Anthony
Reynolds Gallery, London

35 **Five Easy Pieces** 1995
16mm film, video transfer
The artist, courtesy of Anthony
Reynolds Gallery, London

LUCIA NOGUEIRA

36 **Black** 1994
6,000 pieces of a chandelier
Dimensions variable
The artist, courtesy of Anthony
Reynolds Gallery, London
(Edinburgh and Cardiff
showings only)

37 **Bald Fact** 1995
Flagpole, Sellotape
Height: 800 cm
The artist, courtesy of Anthony
Reynolds Gallery, London
(Manchester showing only)

38 **Catch** 1995
Glass, castors
4 x 82 x 62 cm
The artist, courtesy of Anthony
Reynolds Gallery, London

39 **Pinocchio** 1995
Steel, gloss paint, glass, cast iron
72 x 71 x 48 cm
The artist, courtesy of Anthony
Reynolds Gallery, London

40 **Step** 1995
Oriental carpet, broken glass
Approximately 285 x 152 cm
The artist, courtesy of Anthony
Reynolds Gallery, London

CHRIS OFILI

41 **Painting with shit on it** 1993
Acrylic paint, oil paint, polyester
resin, elephant dung on canvas
183 x 122 cm
Courtesy of The British Council

42 **Rara & Mala** 1994
Acrylic paint, oil paint, polyester
resin, elephant dung on canvas
183 x 122 cm
Courtesy of McGuinness Finch

43 **Bag of Shit** 1995
Elephant dung, brown paper
shopping bag
Approximately 1.5 kg
Courtesy of Osterwalder's Art
Office, Hamburg

44 **Ongley** 1995
Oil paint, polyester resin,
elephant dung on linen
122 x 92 cm
Courtesy of Victoria Miro Gallery,
London

45 **Untitled** 1995
Mixed media on linen
Dimensions unknown
Courtesy of the artist

JULIE ROBERTS

46 **Dentist Chair/Leather
19th Century** 1995
Oil and acrylic on canvas
153 x 153 cm
Courtesy of the artist

47 **Operating Table** 1995
Oil and acrylic on canvas
183 x 183 cm
Courtesy of the artist

48 **Push Chair (Special Needs)**
1995
Oil and acrylic on canvas
153 x 153 cm
Courtesy of the artist

49 **Restraining Coat (Female 2)**
1995
Oil and acrylic on canvas
153 x 153 cm
Courtesy of the artist

50 **Single Body (World War 1)** 1995
Oil and acrylic on canvas
183 x 183 cm
Courtesy of the artist

51 **Table (Draped chiffon)** 1995
Oil and acrylic on canvas
183 x 183 cm
Courtesy of the artist

BRIDGET SMITH

52 **Screen One** 1991
C-type print on MDF
183 x 183 cm
Courtesy of the artist

53 **Curzon** 1995
C-type print on MDF
183 x 183 cm
Courtesy of the artist

54 **Empire (Blue)** 1995
C-type print on MDF
183 x 183 cm
Courtesy of the artist

55 **Odeon (Blue)** 1995
C-type print on MDF
183 x 183 cm
Courtesy of Private Collection

56 **Odeon (Green)** 1995
C-type print on MDF
183 x 183 cm
Courtesy of the artist

57 **Premier** 1995
C-type print on MDF
183 x 183 cm
Courtesy of the artist

GEORGINA STARR

58 **Visit to a Small Planet** 1995
Video installation
Components: The Being Blue
Cubicle, The Invisibility Cubicle,
The Mind Reading Cubicle,
The Ravioli Cubicle, Trailer video
projection, Cat Conversation video
The artist, courtesy of Anthony
Reynolds Gallery, London

KERRY STEWART

59 **Drowned Dog** 1995
Fibreglass, rubber
Length: 100 cm
Courtesy of Stephen Friedman
Gallery, London
(Edinburgh and Cardiff
showings only)

Kerry Stewart
(in collaboration with Ana Genoves)
60 **Man in Love** 1995
Painted fibreglass
Height: 170 cm
Courtesy of Stephen Friedman
Gallery, London

61 **Myron** 1995
Glazed (white) ceramic
Height: 170 cm
Courtesy of Stephen Friedman
Gallery, London

62 **Party Here Tonight** 1995
Neon
100 x 300 x 1.5 cm
Courtesy of Stephen Friedman
Gallery, London

MARCUS TAYLOR

63 **Untitled (Abstract 1)** 1991
Clear acrylic sheet
148 x 148 x 52 cm
Courtesy of Saatchi Collection,
London

64 **Untitled (Quadruple Fridge)** 1991
Clear acrylic sheet
156 x 280 x 54.5 cm
Courtesy of Saatchi Collection,
London

65 **Untitled (Model for a Diving
Pool 2)** 1994
Clear acrylic sheet
185 x 201 x 122 cm
Courtesy of Jay Jopling, London

SAM TAYLOR-WOOD

66 **Killing Time** 1994
Video installation
Dimensions variable
Commissioned by The Showroom,
courtesy of Jay Jopling, London

67 **Brontosaurus** 1995
Video projection and sound
Courtesy of Jay Jopling, London

MARK WALLINGER

68 **Regard a Mere Mad Rager** 1993
Video monitor, mirror
Dimensions variable
The artist, courtesy of Anthony
Reynolds Gallery, London

69 **Royal Ascot** 1994
Video installation for 4 monitors
Dimensions variable
The artist, courtesy of Anthony
Reynolds Gallery, London

70 **Half-Brother (Jupiter Island/
Precocious)** 1994/95
Oil on canvas
2 panels, each 230 x 150 cm
Courtesy of Collection
Vanhaerents, Torhout, Belgium

71 **Half-Brother (Unfuwain-
Nashwan)** 1994/95
Oil on canvas
2 panels, each 230 x 150 cm
The artist, courtesy of Anthony
Reynolds Gallery, London

72 **Oh No He's Not, Oh Yes He is**
1995
Pantomime costume, fibreglass
resin
177 x 132 x 58 cm
The artist, courtesy of Anthony
Reynolds Gallery, London

73 **Self portrait as Emily Davison**
1995
Colour photograph on aluminium,
1 of an edition of 3
89 x 137 cm
The artist, courtesy of Anthony
Reynolds Gallery, London

GILLIAN WEARING

74 **Signs that say what you want them to say and not signs that say what someone else wants you to say** 1992/93
Cibachrome on aluminium
30 x 17 x 1 cm
Courtesy of Maureen Paley/
Interim Art

75 **Take Your Top Off** 1993
Cibachrome prints on aluminium
3 panels, 73.5 x 99 cm
Courtesy of Maureen Paley /
Interim Art

76 **Confess all on video. Don't worry you will be in disguise. Intrigued? Call Gillian . . .** 1994
Video for single monitor
Courtesy of Maureen Paley/
Interim Art

77 **I'd like to teach the world to sing (bottles)** 1995
Video projection with sound
Dimensions variable
Courtesy of Maureen Paley/
Interim Art

JANE AND LOUISE WILSON

78 **Hypnotic Suggestion "505"** 1993
Video installation
366 x 274 cm
Courtesy of the artists

79 **Attic** 1995
C-type print on plywood
198 x 201 cm
Courtesy of the artists

80 **Den** 1995
C-type print on plywood
183 x 183 cm
Courtesy of the artists

81 **Red Room** 1995
C-type print on plywood
213 x 213 cm
Courtesy of the artists

HERMIONE WILTSHIRE

82 **My Touch** 1993
Glass, cibachrome, silicon glue
and aluminium
200 x 100 x 30-40 cm
Courtesy of Arts Council
Collection

83 **Two Points of Speech in Sight** 1993
Cibachromes, glass and plaster
Each 50 x 50 x 10 cm
Courtesy of Fritz and Helga
Kleiner, Graz

84 **Seamen II** 1994
Toned black and white
photographs, glass
Dimensions variable
Courtesy of Galerie Eugen Lendl,
Graz

85 **Casanova** 1995
Computer animation
Dimensions variable
Courtesy of the artist

CATHERINE YASS

86 **Corridors** 1995
8 photographic transparencies,
light boxes
Each 86 x 70 x 14 cm
Courtesy of the Public Art
Development Trust